GOOD HOUSEKEEPING

CROCHET DESIGNS

GOOD HOUSEKEEPING

CROCHET DESIGNS

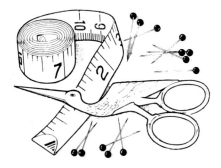

EBURY PRESS

Art Editors
Sue Storey
Patrick McLeavey

Editor
Melanie Miller

Managing Editor
Amy Carroll

Good Housekeeping Crochet Designs
was conceived, edited and designed by
Dorling Kindersley Limited, 9 Henrietta Street, London WC2E 8PS

First published in Great Britain in 1984 by
Ebury Press, National Magazine House,
72 Broadwick Street, London W1V 2BP

Copyright © 1984 by Dorling Kindersley Limited

The expression GOOD HOUSEKEEPING as used in the title of this
book is the trade mark of The National Magazine Company Limited
and The Hearst Corporation, registered in the United Kingdom
and the USA, and other principal countries in the world, and is the
absolute property of The National Magazine Company Limited and
The Hearst Corporation. The use of this trade mark other than with
the express permission of The National Magazine Company Limited
or the Hearst Corporation is strictly prohibited.

All rights reserved. No part of this publication may
be reproduced, stored in retrieval system, or
transmitted in any form or by any means,
electronic, mechanical, photocopying, recording
or otherwise, without the prior written permission
of the copyright owners.

ISBN 0 85223 318 3

Printed and bound in Italy

Contents

Introduction 6

Basic Techniques 7

Abbreviations 20

Squares 21

Hexagons 45

Triangles 59

Circles and Octagons 63

Fillers and Motifs 79

Fruit and Flowers 85

Animals and Objects 91

Index 95

Introduction

Crochet is one of the most versatile and satisfying handicrafts. All that is needed to produce beautiful, creative and original articles is a hook and some yarn. It appeals to both the novice and the expert alike as the basic techniques are easy to master, and all stitches are variations on a few basics. Yet the permutations are endless, so experienced handicrafters can try all manner of elaborate combinations.

As with other textiles, the origins of crochet are difficult to trace. The technique of crochet appears to have travelled extensively, early samples of it have been found in all corners of the globe — in the Far East, Near East, Africa, Europe, South and North America. These early examples fall into two distinctly different categories: either the crochet has been worked on fine hooks with fine yarns, thus producing a delicate open, lacy fabric, or it has been worked with thicker yarn on large hooks to form a dense fabric. The denser type of crochet was used by the Chinese to make three-dimensional sculptural dolls; the Africans used it for making caps for their chieftains; the Turks used it for making hats, and in Scotland it was used for caps and heavy cloaks.

The more delicate, lace-like form of crochet originated in Italy in the sixteenth century where it was worked by nuns to make church trimmings and vestments, hence the name for it at that time of nun's lace. It was made from very fine cotton yarn on the finest crochet hooks. The technique spread to Spain and to Ireland where it was also worked by nuns for the church.

Nowadays the two different kinds of crochet overlap. Many different types of yarn can be used to give different effects — fine cotton and silks will produce a delicate, cobwebby fabric, reminiscent of Victorian handiwork, chunky yarn can be used for warm, hardwearing garments and household articles. Crochet is not limited to ordinary wool and cotton yarn — any thin, pliable medium may be used. For interesting textures raffia, string or ribbons can be used on their own or mixed with other, more conventional yarns. Experiment with different yarns in the same shade for interesting and unusual results — try combining mohair and slub cotton, or lurex and string.

When making articles from several pieces of crochet, the scope for imaginative design is limitless. A riot of different colours can be used in one article at random, using up scraps of leftover yarn, or a carefully planned design may be worked out, perhaps using subtle shades and texture changes. Simple designs may be as effective as more complex, elaborately planned patterns. One of the beauties of crochet is its versatility — thick yarn and a big hook can quickly produce a bright, bold cushion, or hours of work can go into creating an heirloom bedspread or tablecloth using one of the lace patterns.

BASIC TECHNIQUES

HOOKS

Crochet hooks are machine-made, usually from plastic-coated aluminium or steel. They are made in a range of sizes, conforming to the International Standard Range (ISR), from 0.60, for fine cottons, to 10.00, for working very thick rug yarn. Since the hooks do not hold stitches but hold only the working loop, they are all made to a standard length.

WHICH YARN?

Choose the most appropriate yarn, hook and stitch pattern to suit your special needs. Generally, very fine yarns and hooks are used for delicate lacy effects, medium-weights for more practical fabrics, heavy-weights for warmth and hard-wearing qualities. If you are making something which needs frequent laundering, choose a machine-washable yarn.

YARNS

In addition to a very wide range of specially-produced crochet threads, most yarns that are manufactured for knitting, knotting and weaving can be used.

Yarn describes any thread spun from natural fibres such as wool, cotton, linen, silk, or synthetics.

Ply indicates the number of spun single threads which have been twisted together to produce a specific yarn. Single threads may be spun to any thickness so that ply does not refer to a standard thickness of yarn, although the terms 2-, 3- and 4-ply are often used to describe yarns of a recognised thickness. In this book the term "medium-weight" is used instead of "4-ply".

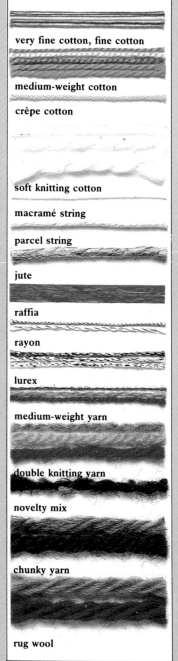

very fine cotton, fine cotton

medium-weight cotton

crêpe cotton

soft knitting cotton

macramé string

parcel string

jute

raffia

rayon

lurex

medium-weight yarn

double knitting yarn

novelty mix

chunky yarn

rug wool

HOLDING THE HOOK AND YARN

Shown below are two different ways of holding the hook and yarn, however these methods are not definitive. The right way is the way you find comfortable and easy, and which results in crochet that is regular and even.

THREADING YARN

Threading the yarn through the fingers is important as this helps to give extra tension, controlling the yarn while allowing it to flow easily from hand to hook. If you are left-handed the method is the same.

Threading yarn around the little finger

Pass the working end of yarn around the little finger, over the next finger, under the middle finger and finish with it resting over the forefinger.

Threading yarn over the little finger

Pass the working end of yarn over the little finger, under the next 2 fingers and finish with it resting over the forefinger.

HOLDING THE HOOK

The crochet hook can be held in either the knife or the pencil position. Both ways are equally good and the choice depends on which position feels most comfortable in the hand.

The pencil position

1 *Hold the hook in the right hand like a pencil. If you are left-handed hold the hook in the same way, but in the left hand.*

2 *Prepare to make the first chain by drawing the yarn from the left forefinger with the hook through the slip loop.*

The knife position

1 *Hold the hook in the right hand like a knife. If you are left-handed hold the hook in the same way, but in the left hand.*

2 *Prepare to make the first chain by drawing the yarn from the left forefinger with the hook through the slip loop.*

THE FOUNDATION CHAIN

To begin crochet, a slip loop is placed on the hook. This is a working loop and is never counted as a stitch. Stitches are made by pulling one loop through another to form a foundation chain upon which the next row or round is worked.

CHAIN STITCH (ch)

1 *Hold back with slip loop in RH, twist hook under and over yarn.*

2 *Draw yarn through slip loop on hook.*

A length of chain sts.

DOUBLE CHAIN STITCH (dch)

1 *Make slip loop and work 2 ch, insert hook into 1st ch, yarn round hook (yrh), draw loop through.*

2 *Yarn round hook, draw through both loops on hook. Repeat steps 1 and 2.*

Use dchs for firm edge.

FINISHING OFF

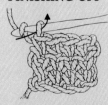 

1 *Complete final st and cut yarn about 15cm from work. Pull through last loop and tighten.*

2 *Thread loose end into yarn needle and darn into back of work.*

COUNTING

Count dc as above. In trebles count 1 upright as 1 st. Count 1 ch between 2 tr as 3 sts.

TURNING CHAINS (t-ch)

Extra chains are worked at the end of a row before turning to bring the hook to the correct depth of the stitch being worked, so that the first stitch can be made evenly.

Table giving number of turning chains required for each stitch

double crochet: 1 turning chain
half treble: 2 turning chains
treble: 3 turning chains
double treble: 4 turning chains
triple treble: 5 turning chains

BASIC STITCHES

Each stitch gives a different texture and varies in depth, and every row makes a new chain line into which the next row is worked. Where stitches are worked back and forth in rows there is no right or wrong side to the work. *NB:* turning chain (**t-ch**) forms first stitch in row.

SINGLE CROCHET/SLIP STITCH (ss)

1 *Make no. of ch. Insert hook from F to B into 2nd ch from hook.*

2 *Yrh, draw through 2 loops on hook. Repeat steps 1 and 2 to end.*

3 *Make 1 t-ch, turn, insert hook into B of first st of last row.*

DOUBLE CROCHET (dc)

  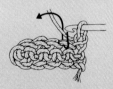

1 *Make ch row. Insert hook into 2nd ch from hook, yrh, draw through.*

2 *Yrh, draw through 2 loops. Repeat steps 1 and 2 to end.*

3 *1 t-ch, turn, insert hook under both loops of 1st st of last row.*

HALF TREBLE (htr)

1 *Make ch row. Yrh and insert into 3rd ch, yrh, draw through.*

2 *Yrh, draw through 3 loops. Cont working htr into every ch to end.*

3 *2 t-chs, turn. Make 1 htr into 1st st of last row, rep to end.*

TREBLE (tr)

  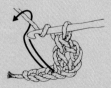

1 *Make ch row. Yrh, insert into 5th ch, yrh, draw 1 loop through.*

2 *Yrh, draw through first 2 lps on hook, rep once more.*

3 *Cont to end, 3 t-ch, turn. Make 1 tr into 2nd st of last row.*

DOUBLE TREBLE (dtr)

1 *Make ch row. Yrh twice, insert into 6th ch from hook, yrh, draw lp through.*

2 *Yrh and draw through first 2 lps on hook. Rep step 2 twice more.*

3 *Cont to end, make 4 t-ch, turn. Make first dtr into 2nd st of row below.*

TRIPLE TREBLE (tr tr)

 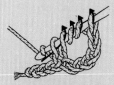 

1 *Make ch row. Yrh 3 times, insert into 7th ch from hook, yrh, draw loop through.*

2 *Yrh and draw through first 2 lps on hook. Rep this step 3 times more.*

3 *Cont to end, make 5 t-ch, turn. Make first tr tr into 2nd st of row below.*

OPENWORK STITCHES

Openwork mesh patterns are formed by missing stitches and working chains over the spaces left; the simplest way to make lacy crochet. Various patterns can be made by altering the combination of stitches and spaces.

Simple openwork
Work 1 tr, 2ch, miss 2 ch in previous row, 1 tr into next ch. Rep to end.

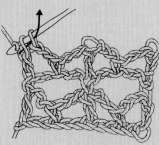

Bar and lattice
1 tr, 3 ch, miss 2 ch in row below, 1 dc into next ch, 3 ch, miss 2 ch. Rep to end.

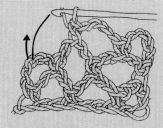

Simple net ground
Work 1 dc into 5th ch of row below, 5 ch, rep to end.

11

BASIC STITCH VARIATIONS

Interesting variations to the basic stitches are made by inserting the hook into different parts of the stitch below and twisting the yarn in different ways.

Crossed double crochet
Work as for dc but take hook over yarn and draw loop through.

Working into half of stitch below
For RS ridge, insert hook into back of st in row below; into front of st for WS ridge.

Working between stitches
Insert hook into space between 2 sts in row below.

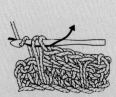

Working into stitches 2 rows below
Insert hook front to back between 2 sts, 2 rows below.

Working into chain space
Insert hook into space between ch sts in row below.

Working a raised effect
Insert hook from front around st below. For indented effect, insert hook from back.

TEXTURED STITCHES

Textures are created by working into the same stitch several times, as in bobble patterns, or by wrapping the yarn around the hook several times before drawing through, as in bullion stitch.

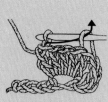

Bobble stitch
5 tr into next st, withdraw hook, insert into 1st tr, pick up lp, draw through.

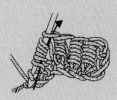

Bullion stitch
Yrh several times, insert hook into ch, yrh, draw through, yrh, draw through all loops.

Cabling around stitch
Yrh, insert hook from back to front around tr in row below, work 1 tr.

12

WORKING IN THE ROUND

Working in the round instead of in rows means that the foundation row of chains is made into a circle or ring, and the crochet stitches are then worked from this circle in a continuous round without turning and working back and forth. Many different shapes can be made from this simple foundation ring: round medallions are made by increasing evenly around the circle; square medallions are made by increasing at four regular intervals; hexagons are made by increasing at six regular intervals, and octagons are made by increasing at eight regular intervals. The medallions can be plain, lace or relief, in one solid colour or a mixture of shades. Medallions usually start with a foundation ring of chains.

Single chain ring

Make a foundation chain to required length and then close ring with a slip stitch into the first chain.

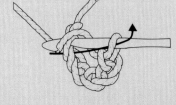

Double crochet ring

If a large number of chains is needed for a medallion, work the ring in double crochet.

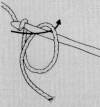
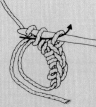
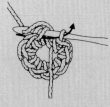

1 *Make a circle with yarn as shown. Insert hook, yrh, draw through circle, yrh, draw through loop.*

2 *Work required number of dc around circle and over both strands.*

3 *Pull loose end firmly to draw circle together. Close ring with a slip stitch.*

Beginning a round

In many of the patterns, the first instruction in round 1 is to chain 1, 2, 3 or more. These chains bring the hook up to the height of the stitches which will then be made into the ring. Although they do not resemble a stitch, these chains are the equivalent of the first stitch of the round. For example:

Round 1 3ch, 11tr into ring.

To allow room for subsequent stitches to fit into the ring, slide the stitches along the ring.

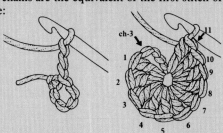

Ending a round

When all the stitches of a round have been made, the first and last stitches are joined with a slip stitch.

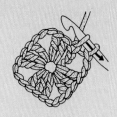

Insert the hook into the third (top) chain of the initial ch-3, pull through a loop, pull the new loop through the loop on the hook, thereby making a slip stitch.

COLOURWORK MEDALLIONS

Colourwork medallions are composed of two or more colours. As well as being decorative, they are an economic way of using up odd scraps of yarn. In colourwork medallions, new colours are added at the beginning of rounds. When breaking off the old yarn at the end of a round and joining in the new colour, secure the ends carefully.

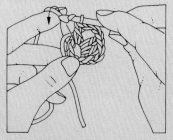

Securing loose end on first round
On first round of medallion, work stitches over loose end.

Securing loose ends on subsequent rounds
When joining in new colours on subsequent rounds work several stitches over loose ends of new and old yarn. When medallion is completed trim ends.

Joining in new colours

There are several different ways of joining in new yarn, two of which are shown below. The exact place where new yarn should be joined is indicated in the pattern instructions.

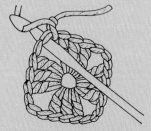

1 *Insert end of new yarn through space where second round is to begin. Make a knot by tying the two ends together.*

2 *Tighten knot, leaving an end of yarn about 7cm long, and have knot fall at far right corner of space. Insert hook into space and pull through a loop. Continue working next round.*

Make a slip knot in the new yarn, leaving an end of yarn about 7cm long. Insert hook into loop then insert hook into space indicated in medallion instructions, pull through another loop. Work a slip stitch, pulling new loop through original loop on hook. Continue working next round.

BLOCKING

Depending on the type of yarn used, crochet medallions may need to be blocked. Individual pieces may be blocked before being sewn together, or a completed project may be blocked after it has been joined.

Place the crochet right side down on a padded surface or ironing board. Pin evenly around the edges. Using a damp cloth and a warm iron, (or as instructed on the ball band), press lightly and evenly, lifting the iron up and down, not to and fro. Do not let the full weight of the iron rest on the crochet. Leave the crochet to cool, and then remove the pins.

Blocking lace and relief crochet

Depending on the intended use of the article, lace designs may be starched before being blocked. Relief crochet should be placed face down over a thick, heavy towel, so that the raised texture of the work is not flattened.

Joining completed medallions together

Depending on the finish required, there are several different ways of joining medallions together.

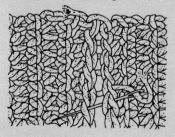

Woven seam

For a very neat, almost invisible seam, lay the medallions wrong side up with edges touching. Thread a needle with matching yarn and weave it loosely around centres of the edge stitches of both pieces.

Sewn seam

Place one medallion on top of another, with right sides together. Thread a needle with matching yarn and oversew the edge stitches of both medallions together.

Double crochet seam

Place one medallion on top of another, with right sides together. Insert the hook from front to back through the edges of both medallions, yrh and draw through, work 1dc in the usual way and then insert the hook into the next stitch along ready to make the next dc.

Slip-stitched seam

Place one medallion on top of another, with right sides together. Insert the hook from front to back through the edge stitches of both pieces, yrh and draw through. Work one ss in the usual way, then insert the hook into the next stitch along, ready to make the next ss.

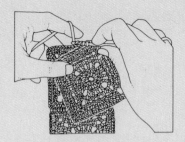

Joining as you go

When making squares, hexagons or octagons, sometimes the second medallion may be joined to the first while working the last round of the second. Specific instructions are given with the patterns. Subsequent medallions may be joined on one or more sides.

Fillers

After circles or octagons, have been joined together, quite large spaces may be left between them. These spaces can be filled with small filler designs. Instructions for these are given with some patterns, or one of the small motifs from the fillers and motifs section may be used.

BORDERS
Double crochet border

After all the medallions have been joined together, the edge can be finished off with one or more rounds of double crochet.

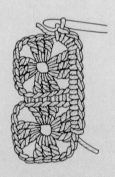

Attach a matching or contrasting yarn to the edge of the piece. Insert the hook from front to back through the edge. Yrh and draw through. Work a double crochet and then continue evenly along the edge, working a dc in every stitch or in every other stitch. In the corner stitch or space, work three dc. At the end of the round, join with a ss into the first dc.

Fringed border

Before adding a fringe there must be a border of one or two rows of double crochet.

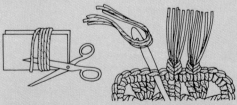

1 *Wind yarn around a carboard gauge which is the desired depth of the completed fringe. Cut ends at one side.*

2 *Fold 3 or 4 strands in half, insert hook in stitch and pull the loop of the strands through the stitch.*

3 *Pull the strands through the loop, and then, to tighten the knot, pull the strands away from the edge.*

CALCULATING THE NUMBER OF MEDALLIONS REQUIRED

Use this method for working out the number of squares, circles, octagons or hexagons required.

1. Decide the length and width you'd like the finished article to be.
2. Crochet one medallion in the yarn you intend to use, then measure the width of the finished medallion.

3. Divide the length of the blanket, cushion, or whatever it is you are going to make by the width of the medallion, then divide the width of your proposed article by the width of the medallion.

4. Multiply these two figures together, and the resulting figure is the number of medallions you require.

Example

To make a blanket measuring 150cm long by 105cm wide, using a medallion 15cm wide:

150 ÷ 15 = 10
105 ÷ 15 = 7
7 × 10 = 70

So total number of medallions required is 70.

SUGGESTED SIZES

Blankets
Suggested approximate sizes:
90cm × 120cm, 120cm × 160cm, 150cm × 200cm.

Tablecloths
Take the measurements from an existing tablecloth, or drape a sheet over the table and take the appropriate measurements from that.

Bedspreads
Take the measurements from an existing bedspread, or drape a sheet over the bed and take the appropriate measurements from that.

Cushions
Can be round or square, any size from 25cm to 50cm across.

Place mats
Round or square, 20cm to 30cm across; rectangular, 20cm to 30cm wide by 30cm to 45cm long.

SUGGESTED PATTERNS

Crochet medallions may be joined together in an infinite number of ways to produce blankets, bedspreads, cushions, tablecloths, place mats, coasters, rugs, shawls, pram covers, bags, or other household or personal objects. The medallions may be joined together at random, or a uniform pattern may be designed. Some suggestions for the layout of medallions are shown overleaf.

SQUARES AND OCTAGONS

HEXAGONS AND CIRCLES

SIZE GUIDE

Each pattern includes information as to the size of the hook and the type of yarn used to produce the particular medallion illustrated. By using thicker or thinner yarn, or a larger or smaller hook, the size of the medallion can be varied.

HOOK AND YARN GUIDE

0.60mm	very fine cotton	4.00	double knitting
0.75		4.50	yarn, mohair
1.00		5.00	
1.25		5.50	
		6.00	
1.25	fine cotton and	6.00	Aran-type, double
1.50	equivalent yarn	7.00	double yarn
1.75		8.00	
2.00			
2.50			
2.50	medium-weight	8.00	chunky, heavy-
3.00	yarn	9.00	weight yarn
3.50		10.00	
4.00			

ABBREVIATIONS

alt	alternate(ly)	**pc**	picot
B	back	**rem**	remain(ing)
beg	beginning	**rep**	repeat
ch(s)	chain(s)	**RS**	right side
cl	cluster	**rnd**	round
cont	continu(e)(ing)	**RTB**	round treble back
dec	decreas(e)(ing)	**RTF**	round treble front
dc	double crochet	**ss**	slip stitch
dch(s)	double chain(s)	**sp(s)**	space(s)
dtr	double treble	**st(s)**	stitch(es)
F	front	**tog**	together
gr(s)	group(s)	**tr**	treble
htr	half treble	**tr tr**	triple treble
inc	increas(e)(ing)	**t-ch(s)**	turning chain(s)
lp(s)	loop(s)	**WS**	wrong side
no.	number	**yrh**	yarn round hook

A star * shown in a pattern row denotes that the stitches shown after this sign must be repeated from that point.

Round brackets ( ), enclosing a particular stitch combination, denote that the stitch combination must be repeated in the order shown.

Round brackets at the end of a round, enclosing a number of stitches, denote the total number of stitches worked in that round.

Hyphens refer to those stitches which have already been made but which will be used as the base for the next stitch, eg., you would work 2tr into 2-ch sp, by making 2 trebles into the space created by the chain stitches worked in the previous row.

SQUARES

Squares are the most versatile of the basic shapes. It is easy to join them together and they can be made into a vast range of articles, from cushion covers, bags and scarves, to bedspreads and tablecloths. One of the most traditional crochet patterns is the granny, or Afghan square, p.44. This design can be made into a striking blanket when individual squares are worked with carefully graded bright colours at the centre, and edged and joined in one dark colour, to give the effect of stained glass windows.

Tudor rose

Size No. 3.50 crochet hook and medium-weight yarn produce a square 6.5cm across.

Materials and uses Use fine, soft, machine-washable yarn for a baby's blanket, or multi-coloured chunky yarn for a rug.

Using A, make 6ch and join into a ring with a ss into first ch.
Round 1 2ch, 1tr into ring, (1ch, 4tr in ring) 3 times, 1ch, 2tr into ring.
Round 2 Ss to first 1ch space, (2ch, 2tr, 2ch, 3tr) in same space, (3tr, 2ch, 3tr) in each of next 3 1ch spaces, ss in top of 2ch. Break off A.

Round 3 Joining B to first 2ch space, (3ch, 3dtr, 3ch, 4dtr) in first 2ch space, (4dtr, 3ch, 4dtr) in each of next 3 2ch spaces, ss in top of 2ch. Break off B.
Round 4 Join in C to ss, 1dc in each st and 4dc in each 3ch space to end of round, ss in first dc. Fasten off.

Rainbow

Size No. 4.00 crochet hook and double knitting wool produce a square 11cm across.

Materials and Uses Use oddments of brightly coloured chunky wool for cheerful cushion covers, or make a bedspread from novelty bouclé or tweedy yarn.

This square uses 6 colours, A, B, C, D, E and F.

Using A, make 4ch, and join into a ring with a ss into first ch.

Round 1 4ch, 3dtr into ring, (2ch, 4dtr into ring) 3 times, 2ch, join with a ss to 4th of first 4ch. Break off A and turn.

Round 2 (RS) Join in B to any 2ch space, 2dc into same space, (1dc into each of next 4sts, 2dc, 2ch, 2dc into corner 2ch space) 3 times, 1dc into each of next 4sts, 2dc into same space as join, 2ch, join with a ss to first dc. Break off B and turn.

Round 3 Join in C to first dc after a 2ch space, 3ch, 1tr into 2ch space before join, *(miss next dc, 1tr into next dc, 1tr into missed dc) 3 times, miss 1dc, 1tr into next 2ch space, 1tr into missed dc, 1tr into next dc, 1tr into 2ch space before last tr; repeat from * 3 times omitting last 2tr at end of last repeat; join with a ss to 3rd of first 3ch. Break off C and turn.

Round 4 Join in D to same place as ss of last round, 3ch, 2tr into same space, (1ch, 3tr into next tr, 1tr into each of next 8tr, 3tr into next tr) 4 times omitting 3tr at end of last repeat, join with a ss to 3rd of first 3ch. Break off D and turn.

Round 5 Join in E to first tr after any 1ch space, 1dc into same place as join, 1dc into next tr, *(1dtr into next tr, then bending dtr in half to form bobble on RS of square work 1dc into next tr, 1dc into next tr) 4 times, 3tr into corner 1ch space, 1dc into each of next 2tr; repeat from * 3 times omitting 2dc at end of last repeat, join with a ss to first dc. Break off E and turn.

Round 6 Join in F to first dc of any side, (1dc into each st to centre tr of 3tr at corner, 3dc into corner tr) 4 times, 1dc in next tr, join with a ss to first dc. Fasten off.

Daisy square

Size No. 4.00 crochet hook and double knitting wool produce a square 7cm across.

Materials and uses Make a pram cover from brightly coloured cotton crêpe, or use oddments of double knitting or chunky yarn for a hot water bottle cover.

This square uses 3 colours, A, B and C.

Using A, make 4ch and join into a ring with a ss into first ch.

Round 1 1ch, 8dc into ring, join with a ss to first ch. Break off A.

Round 2 Join in B to any dc, ss into same place as join, (4ch, leaving last loop of each dtr on hook work 2dtr into same place as last ss, yrh and draw through all three loops, 4ch, ss into same place as last ss — petal worked —, ss into next dc) 8 times, working ss at end of last repeat in same dc as join. Break off B.

Round 3 Join in C to top of any petal, (1dc into top of petal, 3ch, 1dc into top of next petal, 5ch) 4 times, join with a ss to first dc.

Round 4 1dc into same place as ss, (1dc into each of next 3ch, 1dc into next dc, 1dc into each of next 2ch, 3dc into next ch — corner worked — 1dc into each of next 2ch, 1dc into next dc) 4 times, omitting 1dc at end of last repeat, join with a ss to first dc. Fasten off.

Bermuda triangle

Size No. 3.00 crochet hook and medium-weight wool produce a square 9.5cm across (row 4 repeated once).

Materials and uses Use pretty pastel colours and soft yarn for a baby's shawl or blanket, or join nine or more for cushion covers.

This design uses 5 colours, A, B, C, D and E.

Row 1 Using A, 4ch, 2tr in 4th ch from hook, 5ch, turn.

Row 2 2tr in 4th ch from hook, 1ch, 3tr in 3rd ch of 3-ch, 5ch, turn.

Row 3 2tr in 4th ch from hook, 1ch, 3tr in 1-ch space, 1ch, 3tr in 3rd ch of 3-ch, 5ch, turn.

Row 4 2tr in 4th ch from hook, (1ch, 3tr) in each 1-ch space across, 1ch, 3tr in 3rd ch of 3-ch, 5ch, turn.

Repeat row 4 as many times as you wish. Make 3 more motifs, with B, C and D, each having the same number of rows. Sew them together to form a square. Using E, work double crochet edging all around.

Star bright

Size No. 3.50 crochet hook and medium-weight wool produce a square 6cm across.

Materials and uses Make a bright, warm bedspread from oddments of chunky yarn, or use double knitting wool for a tea cosy or a hot water bottle cover.

This design uses 2 colours, A and B. Using A, make 6ch and join into a ring with a ss into first ch.

Round 1 1ch, *dc in ring, 3ch, dtr in ring, 3ch, dtr in ring, 3ch; repeat from * 3 more times, ending with ss in first dc made (4 petals). Break off A.

Round 2 Join in B to a dtr following the 3-ch at centre of a petal, 1ch, dc in same dtr, *dc in top st of next 3-ch, 2tr in dc between petals, dc in top st of next 3-ch, dc in next dtr, dc in next ch, 3ch, miss 1ch, dc in next ch, dc in next dtr; repeat from * around, ending with 3ch, dc in ch preceding first dc made, join with a ss to first dc.

Round 3 3ch (to count as tr), tr in each st to corner 3-ch, in corner 3-ch make tr, 3ch and tr. Continue thus around, join with a ss to 3rd st of 3-ch first made. Fasten off.

Lazy daisy

Size No. 4.00 crochet hook and double knitting yarn produce a square 8cm across.
Materials and uses Use silky yarn for a shawl, or acrylic yarn for a luncheon set.

This square uses 2 colours, A and B. Using A, make 10ch and join into a ring with a ss into first ch.
Round 1 (10ch, dc into ring) 12 times. Break off A.
Round 2 Join in B to any 10-ch loop, 3ch, (2tr, 2ch, 3tr) in same loop, *3htr in each of next 2 loops, (3tr, 2ch, 3tr) in next loop; repeat from * twice more, work 3htr in each of last 2 loops, join with a ss to 3rd ch of 3-ch. Fasten off.

Crossed square

Size No. 3.50 crochet hook and medium-weight cotton produce a square 10.5cm across.
Materials and uses Use slub linen for a bedspread, or use thick chenille for pot holders.

This square uses 2 colours, A and B.
Note *Cluster (cl): work 3tr keeping last loop of each st on hook, draw a loop through all sts on hook.*
Using A, make 8ch and join into a ring with a ss into first ch.
Round 1 2ch, into ring work (1cl, 2ch, 1cl, 5ch) 4 times, join with a ss.
Round 2 2ch, *3tr into 2ch loop (2ch, 1cl, 3ch, 1cl, 2ch) into 5ch loop; repeat from * 3 more times, join with a ss to 2nd of 2ch. Break off A.
Round 3 Join in B to joining ss with a ss and 2ch, *1tr into each tr, 2tr into 2ch loop (2ch, 1cl, 3ch, 1cl, 2ch) into 3ch loop, 2tr into 2ch loop; repeat from * 3 more times, join with a ss.
Round 4 2ch, work as round 3 from * 4 times, ending 1tr into each of last 2tr, join with a ss to 2nd of 2ch.
Round 5 As round 4, ending 1tr into each of last 4tr, join with a ss to 2nd of 2ch. Fasten off.

Arched square

Size No. 3.00 crochet hook and medium-weight cotton produce a square 9cm across.

Materials and uses Use fine cotton for tablecloth insertion and border, or join 9 or more made from medium-weight or double knitting yarn for a cushion cover.

Make 8ch and join into a ring with a ss into first ch.

Round 1 3ch, 2tr into ring, 7ch, (3tr, 7ch) 7 times into ring, join with a ss to top of 3ch.

Round 2 Ss into next 7ch loop, 3ch, 2tr into same loop, 2ch, 3tr into same loop, *7ch, miss next loop, (3tr, 2ch, 3tr) into next loop; repeat from * twice more, 7ch, miss last loop, join with a ss to top of first 3ch.

Round 3 3ch, 1tr into each of next 2tr, *(2tr, 2ch, 2tr) into corner space, 1tr into each of next 3tr, 7ch, 1tr into each of next 3tr; repeat from * twice more, (2tr, 2ch, 2tr) into corner space, 1tr into each of next 3tr, 7ch, join with a ss to top of first 3ch.

Round 4 3ch, 1tr into each of next 4tr, *(2tr, 2ch, 2tr) into corner space, 1tr into each of next 5tr, 4ch, 1dc into missed 7ch loop of round 1 and enclosing chains of 2nd and 3rd rounds, 4ch, 1tr into each of next 5tr; repeat from * 3 more times, omitting last 5tr, join with a ss to top of first 3ch. Fasten off.

Bull's-eye

Size No. 4.00 crochet hook and double knitting yarn produce a square 11cm across.

Materials and uses Make a padded tea cosy or hot water bottle cover from oddments of chunky or double knitting yarn, or use thick acrylic yarn for a quick-drying bath mat.

This square uses 4 colours, A, B, C and D.

Using A, make 4ch and join into a ring with a ss into first ch.

Round 1 3ch, 11tr into ring (12tr), join with a ss to 3rd ch of 3-ch. Break off A.

Round 2 Join in B to any tr, 3ch, tr in same st, work 2tr in each tr around (24tr), join with a ss to 3rd ch of 3-ch. Break off B.

Round 3 Join in C to any tr, 3ch, tr in same st, *tr in next tr, 2tr in next tr; repeat from * around (36tr), join with a ss to 3rd ch of 3-ch. Break off C.

Round 4 Join in D to any tr st, 4ch, 4dtr in same st, *in next 8 sts work tr, 6htr, tr, 5dtr in next st; repeat from * around, join with a ss to 4th ch of 4-ch.

Round 5 3ch, tr in next tr and every tr till corner dtr st (centre dtr of 5-dtr group), *5tr into corner dtr st, tr in every st till next corner dtr; repeat from * around, join with a ss to 3rd ch of 3-ch. Fasten off.

Cart-wheel

Size No. 4.00 crochet hook and medium-weight wool produce a square 9.5cm across.

Materials and uses Use oddments of yarn to make a blanket or a pram cover.

This square uses 3 colours, A, B, and C.

Using A, make 5ch and join into a ring with a ss into first ch.

Round 1 5ch, (dtr in ring, 1ch) 11 times, join with a ss to 4th ch of 5-ch. Break off A.

Round 2 Join in B to any 1-ch space, pull up loop on hook to 1.5cm, make puff st in same space – (yrh, pull up loop in space to 1.5cm) 3 times, yrh and through all 7 loops on hook, 1ch, make another puff st in same place, *(puff st, 1ch, puff st, 1ch) in next space; repeat from * 10 times, join with a ss to top of first puff st. Break

off B (24 puff sts around).

Round 3 Join in C to any 1-ch space, 6ch, dtr in same space, *1ch, tr in next space, (1ch, htr in next space) 3 times, 1ch, tr in next space, 1ch, (dtr, 2ch, dtr) in next space; repeat from * around, working 2 more corners, after last tr, 1ch, join with a ss to 4th ch of 6-ch.

Round 4 Ss into corner 2-ch space, 1ch, *(dc, 3ch, dc) in corner space, (1ch, dc in space after next st) 6 times, 1ch; repeat from * 3 more times, join with a ss to first dc made. Fasten off.

Plain square

Size No. 4.00 crochet hook and medium-weight yarn produce a square 7cm across (3 rounds worked).

Materials and uses Make a blanket from chunky wool or use chenille for a cushion cover.

Make 4ch

Round 1 (1tr, 1ch, 4tr, 1ch, 4tr, 1ch, 4tr, 1ch, 2tr) into the first ch st, ss into top of starting chain.

Round 2 3ch, tr into next tr, (2tr, 1ch, 2dc) into corner st ch, *4tr into 4tr, (2tr, 1ch, 2tr) into corner st; repeat from * twice more, 2tr, join with a ss. Continue in this way, working 1 tr into each tr and working the corners (1tr into corner st ch, 2tr, 1ch, 2tr), until square is the required size. Fasten off.

Wagon wheel

Size No. 3.50 crochet hook and medium-weight wool produce a square 7cm across.

Materials and uses Join four or more for place mats, use individual squares as coasters.

This square uses 2 colours, A and B. Using A, make 6ch and join into a ring with a ss into first ch.

Round 1 2ch, 15tr in ring, join with ss in top of 2ch. Break off A.

Round 2 Join in B to ss, 4ch, *1tr in back loop only of next tr, 2ch; repeat from * to end of round, join with a ss to 2nd st of 4ch. Break off B.

Round 3 Join in A, 5ch, 1dtr in same st, *2ch, 1tr in next tr, 2ch, 1htr in next tr, 2ch, 1 tr in next tr, 2ch, (1dtr, 2ch, 1dtr) in next tr; repeat from * twice more, 2ch, 1tr in next tr, 2ch, 1 htr in next tr, 2ch, 1tr in next tr, 2ch, join with a ss to 3rd st of 5ch.

Round 4 3dc in first space, 1dc in each st, 2dc in each space, 3dc in each corner space to end of round, join with a ss to first st. Fasten off.

Powder puff

Size No. 4.00 crochet hook and medium-weight yarn produce a square 7cm across.

Materials and uses Use machine-washable yarn for a pram cover or baby's blanket, or use chunky yarn and a large hook for a rug.

This square uses 2 colours, A and B. Using A, make 6ch and join into a ring with a ss into first ch.

Round 1 1ch, 8dc into ring, join with a ss to first dc made.

Round 2 Pull up loop on hook to 2cm, (yrh, pull up loop in first dc to 2cm) 4 times, yrh and through all 9 loops on hook, 1ch tightly to fasten st (a puff st made), 4ch, *(yrh, pull up loop in next dc to 2cm) 4 times, yrh and through all 9 loops on hook, 1ch tightly, 2ch, make puff st same way in next dc, 4ch; repeat from * 2 more times, make puff st in last dc, 2ch, join with a ss to top of first puff st. Break off A.

Round 3 Join in B to any 4-ch corner space, 3ch, (2tr, 2ch, 3tr) in same space, *3tr in next space, (3tr, 2ch, 3tr) in next corner 4-ch space; repeat from * 2 times, 3tr in last space, join with a ss to 3rd ch of 3-ch. Fasten off.

Squares and triangles

Size No. 2.50 crochet hook and 3-ply wool produce a square 5cm across.

Materials and uses Make a baby's blanket or shawl from fine, soft, machine-washable yarn, or use oddments of medium-weight cotton for place mats.

This square uses 4 colours, A, B, C and D.

Round 1 Using A, make 4ch, 15tr into 4th ch from hook, join with a ss to top of 4ch. Break off A.

Round 2 Join in B to any st, 1dc into same place as join, (miss one st, 5htr into next st, miss one st, 1dc into next st) 4 times omitting 1dc at end of last repeat, join with a ss to first dc. Break off B.

Round 3 Join in C to centre htr of any 5htr group, 1dc into same place as join, (7tr into next dc, 1dc into centre htr of next 5htr group) 4 times omitting 1dc at end of last repeat, join with a ss to first dc. Break off C.

Round 4 Join in D to centre tr of any 7tr group, 1dc into same place as join, (9dtr into next dc, 1dc into centre tr of next 7tr group) 4 times omitting 1dc at end of last repeat, join with a ss to first dc. Fasten off.

Sea green square

Size No. 3.50 crochet hook and medium-weight yarn produce a square 9cm across.

Materials and uses Use leftover scraps of chunky or double knitting yarn for a blanket, or use medium-weight wool for cushion covers.

This square uses 4 colours, A, B, C and D.

Using A, make 6ch and join into a ring with a ss into first ch.

Round 1 3ch, 3tr into ring, (3ch, 4tr) 3 times into ring, 3ch, join with a ss to 3rd of first 3ch. Break off A and turn.

Round 2 (RS) Join in B to any 3ch space, 3ch, 1tr into same space, (1tr into each of next 4tr, 2tr into next 3ch space, 1tr tr into commencing circle between the 4tr groups, 2tr into same space as last 2tr) 4 times omitting 2tr at end of last repeat, join with a ss to 3rd of first 3ch. Break off B and turn.

Round 3 Join in C to any tr tr, 3ch, (1tr into each of next 8tr, 1tr, 3ch, 1tr into next tr tr) 3 times, 1tr into each of last 8tr, 1tr into same place as join, 3ch, join with a ss to 3rd of first 3ch. Break off C and turn.

Round 4 Join in D to any 3ch space, 3ch, 1tr into same space, (1tr into each of next 10tr, 2tr into next 3ch space, 1tr tr around stem of tr tr worked on round 2 inserting hook from right to left from front of work, 2tr into same space as last 2tr) 4 times, omitting 2tr at end of last repeat, join with a ss to 3rd of first 3ch. Fasten off.

Irish lace square

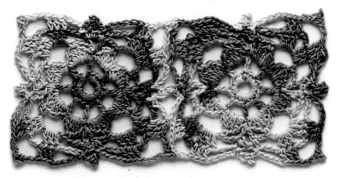

Size No. 1.25 crochet hook and very fine cotton produce a square 5cm across.

Materials and uses Use fine or very fine cotton for tablecloth insertions or borders.

Make 8ch and join into a ring with a ss into first ch.

Round 1 1ch, 15dc into ring, join with a ss to first ch (16dc).

Round 2 5ch to count as first htr and 3ch space, *miss 1dc, 1htr into next dc, 3ch; repeat from * 6 more times, join with a ss to 2nd of first 5ch.

Round 3 (1dc, 1htr, 3tr, 1htr, 1dc) into each ch space to end, join with a ss to the first dc (8 petals).

Round 4 2ch to count as first htr, *3ch, 1dc into 2nd tr of next petal, 6ch, 1dc into 2nd tr of next petal, 3ch, 1htr into space before first dc of next petal, 3ch, 1htr into same space; repeat from * twice more, 3ch, 1dc into 2nd tr of next petal, 6ch, 1dc into 2nd tr of next petal, 3ch, 1htr into space before first dc of next petal, 3ch, join with a ss to 2nd of first 2ch.

Round 5 *4ch, (3tr, 3ch, 3tr) into next 6ch space, 4ch, 1dc into htr, 1dc into 3ch space, 1dc into htr; repeat from * to end, join with a ss to first of first 4ch.

Round 6 *5ch, 1tr into each of next 3tr, 5ch, insert hook into 3rd ch from hook and work 1dc to form picot, 2ch, 1tr into each of next 3tr, 5ch, ss into next dc, 4ch, insert hook into 3rd ch from hook and work 1dc to form picot, 1ch, miss 1dc, ss into next dc; repeat from * to end, join with a ss to first of first 5ch.
Fasten off.

These squares may be crocheted together on the 6th round.

Rounds 1–5 As rounds 1–5 above.

Round 6 5ch, 1tr into each of next 3tr, 2ch, 1dc into corner picot of first square, 2ch, 1tr into each of next 3tr on 2nd square, ss into first of the 5ch after tr of first square, 4ch, ss into next dc of 2nd square, 1ch, 1dc into centre side picot of first square, 1ch, miss 1dc on 2nd square, ss into next dc on 2nd square, 4ch, ss into ch before next 3tr on first square, 1tr into each of next 3tr on 2nd square, 2ch, 1dc into corner picot at end of first square, 2ch, complete round as for first square.

Subsequent squares may be joined in this way along one or more sides.

Square in a square

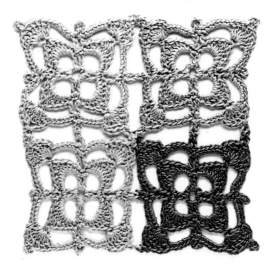

Size No. 2.50 crochet hook and fine cotton produce a square 7cm across.

Material and uses Create a lacy bedspread from medium-weight cotton, or use silky yarn for cushion covers.

Make 8ch and join into a ring with a ss into first ch.

Round 1 3ch, 1tr in ring (6ch, 2tr in ring) 3 times, 6ch, join with a ss to top of 3ch.

Round 2 1dc between 3ch and tr, *(1dc, 1htr, 2tr, 3dtr, 2tr, 1htr, 1dc) in next 6ch space, 1dc between next 2tr; repeat from * 3 more times, omitting 1dc at end of last repeat, join with a ss to first dc.

Round 3 Ss in next dc, 10ch, *miss next 4sts, 1dc in centre dtr, 7ch, miss next 4sts, 1tr in dc, miss next dc, 1tr in next dc, 7ch; repeat from * 3 more times, omitting 1tr and 7ch at end of last repeat, join with a ss to 3rd of 10ch.

Round 4 *6dc in ch space, 4dtr in next dc, 5ch, ss in last st − 1pc

worked − 3dtr in same dc, 6dc in next ch space, 1dc between next 2tr, 1pc; repeat from * 3 more times, join with a ss to first dc. Fasten off. These squares may be crocheted together on the 4th round.

Rounds 1–3 As rounds 1–3 above.

Round 4 *6dc in ch space, 4dtr in next dc, 2ch, ss in corner pc of first square, 2ch, ss in last st on 2nd square, 3dtr in same dc, 6dc in next ch space, 1dc between next 2tr **, 2ch, ss to next pc of first square, 2ch, ss in last st on 2nd square; repeat from * to **, 1pc; repeat from * of round 4 of first square twice, join with a ss to first dc. Fasten off. Subsequent squares may be joined in this way along one or more sides.

Lattice star

Size No. 2.00 crochet hook and fine cotton produce a square 10cm across.

Materials and uses Make a tablecloth from fine cotton, or use very fine cotton for a tablecloth insertion or border.

Wind yarn 10 times round one finger, then slip loop off finger.

Round 1 32dc in ring, join with a ss.

Round 2 8ch, (1tr in next dc, miss 2dc, 1tr in next dc, 5ch) 7 times, 1tr in next dc, join with ss to 3rd of 8ch.

Round 3 *(3dc, 3ch, 3dc) in loop, 1dc between 2tr, 3ch, ss in last dc — pc worked; rep from * 7 more times, working last dc and pc between tr and 3ch, join with a ss to first dc.

Round 4 Ss to 3ch loop, 3dc, (4tr, 3ch, 5tr), *(5tr, 3ch, 5tr) in next 3ch loop; repeat from * 6 times, join with a ss to 3rd of 3ch.

Round 5 Ss to 3ch loop, 1dc in same loop, *8ch, (1dtr, 7ch, 1dtr) in next 3ch loop, 8ch, 1dc in next 3ch loop; repeat from * 3 more times, finishing last repeat ss in first dc.

Round 6 1dc in 1st dc, *pc, 8dc in ch loop, 1dc in dtr, pc, (5dc, pc, 4dc) in next ch loop, 1dc in dtr, pc, 8dc in next ch loop, 1 dc in next dc; repeat from * 3 more times, finishing last repeat ss in first dc. Fasten off. These square may be crocheted together on the 6th round.

Rounds 1–5 As rounds 1–5 above.

Round 6 1dc in first dc, pc, 8dc in next lp, 1dc in next dtr, pc, 5dc in next lp, then work 1ch, 1 dc in a corresponding pc on 1st square, 1ch, ss in last dc on 2nd square — joining pc worked — 4dc in same lp, 1dc in next dtr, joining pc, 8dc in next lp, 1dc in next dc, joining pc, 8dc in next lp, 1dc in next dtr, joining pc, 5dc in next lp, joining pc, 4dc in same lp, complete round as for first square. Subsequent squares may be joined in this way along one or more sides.

Sparkle star

Size 2.50 crochet hook and medium-weight yarn produce a square 7cm across.

Materials and uses Use lurex or other sparkling yarns for festive place mats and coasters, or make a lacy shawl from fine cotton.

This square uses 2 colours, A and B. Using A, make 4ch and join into a ring with a ss into first ch.

Round 1 1ch, 8dc into ring, join with a ss to first dc made.

Round 2 *6ch, dc in 3rd ch from hook, dc in next ch, htr in each of next 2ch, ss in next dc on ring; repeat from * 7 more times. Break off A.

Round 3 Join in B to top of any petal, 5ch, tr in same space, *4ch, ss in top of next petal, 4ch, (tr, 2ch, tr) in top of next petal; repeat from * 2 times,

4ch, ss in top of last petal, 4ch, join with a ss to 3rd ch of 5-ch.

Round 4 *(3dc, 2ch, 3dc) in corner 2-ch space, 4dc in 4-ch space, miss ss, 4dc in next 4-ch space; repeat from * 3 times, join with a ss to first dc made.

Round 5 1ch, dc in joining st and in next 2dc, *3dc in corner 2-ch space, dc in each dc to next corner; repeat from * around, join with a ss to first dc made. Fasten off.

Diamond lattice

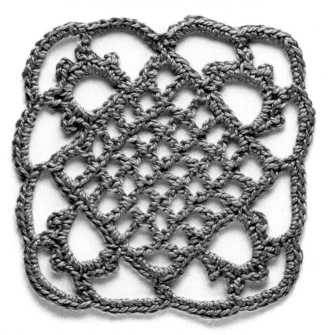

Size No. 3.50 crochet hook and medium-weight cotton produce a square 12cm across.

Materials and uses Make a delicate tablecloth from multi-coloured cotton, or use medium-weight cotton for pretty cushion covers.

Make 23ch.

Row 1 Into 8th ch from hook work 1tr, *2ch, miss 2ch, 1tr into next ch; repeat from * 4 more times, turn (6 spaces).

Row 2 5ch, 1tr into top of next tr, *2ch, 1tr into top of next tr; repeat from * 4 more times, turn.

Rows 3, 4, 5 and 6 As row 2.

Row 7 1ch, 2dc into space, *2dc into each of next 3 spaces, 10ch, turn, 1dc between dc immediately above 2nd tr in from left, turn, into 10ch loop work (2dc, 3ch) 5 times, 2dc into same loop, 2dc into next space to left,

6dc into corner; repeat from * 3 more times ending 3rd repeat with 3dc into corner instead of 6dc, join with a ss to first ch.

Row 8 1ch, *8ch, 1dc into 2nd of 3ch loop round circle, 10ch, 1dc into 4th of 3ch loop round circle, 8ch, 1dc between 3rd and 4th dc in corner space; repeat from * 3 more times, join with a ss to first ch.

Round 9 *8dc into 8ch loop, 10dc into 10ch loop, 8dc into 8ch loop; repeat from * 3 more times, join with a ss to first dc. Fasten off.

Lacy daisy

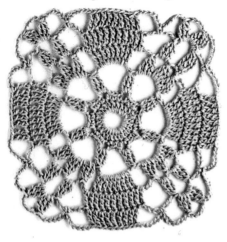

Size No. 3.50 crochet hook and medium-weight cotton produce a square 17cm across.

Materials and uses Use medium-weight silky cotton for a bedspread, or fine cotton for a shawl.

Make 10ch and join into a ring with a ss into first ch.

Round 1 3ch, 23tr in ring, join.

Round 2 Dc in same place as ss, *3ch, dc in next 3dc; repeat from * around, ending with dc in last 2tr, join with a ss to first dc made.

Round 3 Ss in next 3-ch loop, 4ch, holding back on hook the last loop of each dtr make 2dtr in same 3-ch space, thread over and draw through all loops on hook − a 2-tr cluster made −, *7ch, holding back on hook the last loop of each dtr make 3dtr in next 3-ch and complete as for a cluster; repeat from * around, ending with 7ch, join with a ss to top of first cluster.

Round 4 Ss in 7-ch loop, 4ch, in same place as last ss make 2dtr cluster, 4ch, 3dtr cluster, 4ch and 3dtr cluster; *4ch, 9dtr in next 7-ch loop, 4ch, in next 7-ch loop make three 3dtr clusters with 4ch between each cluster; repeat from * around, join last 4ch to top of first cluster.

Round 5 Ss in next 2ch, dc in 4-ch space, 4ch, 2dtr cluster in last dc, *4ch, 3dtr cluster in next 4-ch space, 7ch, dtr in next space, dtr in next 9dtr, dtr in next space, 7ch, 3dtr cluster in next 4-ch space; repeat from * around, join last 7ch to top of first cluster.

Round 6 Ss in next loop, 4ch, 2dtr cluster in same loop, *5ch, 3dtr cluster in same loop, 7ch, dc in next loop, 7ch, miss 1 dtr, dtr in next 9dtr, 7ch, dc in next loop, 7ch, 3dtr cluster in next loop; repeat from * around, join and fasten off.

These squares may be crocheted together on the 6th round.

Rounds 1–5 As rounds 1–5 above

Round 6 Ss in next loop, 4ch, 2dtr cluster in same loop, 2ch, ss in corresponding loop of first square, 2ch, 3dtr cluster back in same place as last cluster on 2nd square, 3ch, dc in next loop on first square, 3ch, dc back in next loop on 2nd square, 3ch, dc in next loop on first square, 3ch, miss 1dtr on 2nd square, dtr in next 4dtr, ss in 5th dtr on first square, dtr in next 5dtr back on 2nd square, and continue as for first square, joining next 3 loops to corresponding loops of first square as first 3 loops were joined. Complete round as for first square.

Subsequent squares may be joined in this way along one or more sides.

Petal square

Size No. 3.50 crochet hook and medium-weight wool produce a square 6.5cm across.

Materials and uses Use odds and ends of yarn to make a multi-coloured blanket, or make a delicate shawl from fine or medium-weight cotton.

This square uses 4 colours, A, B, C and D.

Using A, make 4ch and join into a ring with a ss into first ch.

Round 1 4ch, (tr in ring, 1ch) 7 times, join with a ss to 3rd ch of 4-ch. Break off A (8 spaces around).

Round 2 Join in B to any 1-ch space, 3ch, make cluster st in same space, (yrh, pull up loop in space, yrh and through 2 loops on hook) 3 times, yrh and through all 4 loops on hook, 1ch tightly, 2ch, *make cluster st in next 1-ch space (yrh, pull up loop in space, yrh and through 2 loops on hook) 4 times, yrh and through all 5 loops on hook, 1ch tightly, 2ch;

repeat from * 6 more times, join with a ss to top of first cluster st. Break off B.

Round 3 Join in C to any 2-ch space, (3ch, 2tr, 2ch, 3tr) in same space, *3tr in next space, (3tr, 2ch, 3tr) in next space; repeat from * 2 more times, 3tr in last space, join with a ss to 3rd ch of 3-ch. Break off C.

Round 4 Join in D to any tr on any side of square, dc in same st and in every st till 2-ch corner space, *(dc, 2ch, dc) in corner, dc in every st till next corner 2-ch space; repeat from * around, join with a ss to first dc made. Fasten off.

Flower square

Size No. 4.50 crochet hook and double knitting wool produce a square 17cm across.

Materials and uses Make a bedspread from medium-weight cotton, or sew four squares together to make a cushion cover.

This square uses 2 colours, A and B.
Note *Cluster (cl): Work 3tr keeping last loop of each st on hook, draw a loop through all sts on hook.*
Using A, make 6ch and join into a ring with a ss into first ch.
Round 1 2ch, 23tr into ring, join with a ss to 2nd of 2ch.
Round 2 4ch, 1tr into same ch as ss, 1ch, *miss 2sts, (1tr, 2ch, 1tr) into next st, 1ch; repeat from * 6 more times, join with a ss to 2nd of 4ch.
Round 3 2ch, (1tr, 2ch, 2tr) into first ch space, *1dc into 1ch space, (2tr, 2ch, 2tr) into 2ch space; repeat from * 6 more times, 1dc into last ch space. Break off A.

Round 4 Join in B to next 2ch space with a dc, *7ch, 1dc into next 2ch space, 5ch, 1dc into next 2ch space; repeat from * 3 more times ending with a ss into joining dc instead of dc.
Round 5 2ch, *7tr into 7ch loop (2ch, 1cl, 3ch, 1cl, 2ch) into 5ch loop; repeat from * 3 more times, join with a ss to 2nd of 2ch.
Round 6 2ch, *1tr into each tr, 2tr into 2ch loop, (2ch, 1cl, 3ch, 1cl, 2ch) into 3ch loop, 2tr into 2ch loop; repeat from * 3 more times, join with a ss to 2nd of 2ch.
Round 7 As round 6 but ending 1tr into each of last 2tr, join with a ss to 2nd of 2ch. Fasten off.

Lacy shells

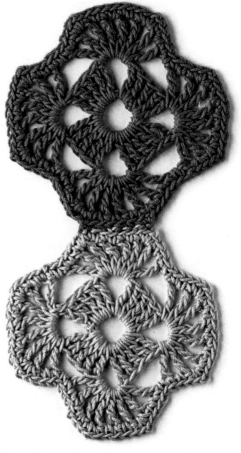

Size No. 3.00 crochet hook and fine cotton produce a square 8cm across (measured diagonally).
Materials and uses Make matching place mats and coasters from medium-weight cotton.

Make 10ch and join into a ring with a ss into first ch.
Round 1 7ch, *5dtr into ring, 3ch; repeat from * 2 times, 4dtr into ring, join with a ss to 4th ch of 7-ch.
Round 2 Ss into corner space, 5ch, (dtr, 1ch) 7 times into same space, *(dtr, 1ch) 8 times into next corner space; repeat from * twice, join with a ss to 4th ch of 5-ch.
Round 3 1ch, dc in same st, dc in next 1-ch space, *dc in next dtr, (dc, 1ch, dc) in next 1-ch space, (dc in next dtr, dc in next 1-ch space) 3 times, dc in next dtr, (dc, 1ch, dc) in next 1-ch space, (dc in next dtr, dc in next 1-ch space) 3 times; repeat from * around, join with a ss to first dc made. Fasten off.
To join Sew corners of squares together.

Lattice square

Size No. 3.50 crochet hook and double knitting yarn produce a square 8.5cm across.

Materials and uses Use a large crochet hook and thick string to make a hard-wearing door mat, or make a blanket from tweedy bouclé yarn.

This square uses 3 colours, A, B and C.

Row 1 Using A, 12ch, tr in 6th ch from hook, *1ch, miss 1ch, tr in next ch; repeat from * 2 times, 4ch, turn.

Row 2 Tr in 2nd tr, *1ch, tr in next tr; repeat from * once, 1ch, tr in 2nd ch on 6-ch loop, 4ch, turn.

Row 3 *Tr in next tr, 1ch; repeat from * 2 times, work last tr in 2nd ch of 4-ch, 4ch, turn.

Row 4 As row 3. Break off A.

Round 1 Join in B to any corner space, (3ch, 2tr, 3ch, 3tr) in same space, *3tr in each of next 2 spaces, (3tr, 3ch, 3tr) in next corner space; repeat from * 2 times, 3tr in each of last 2 spaces, join with a ss to 3rd ch of 3-ch. Break off B.

Round 2 Join in C to any 3-ch corner space, (dc, 2ch, dc) in same space, *dc in every tr to next corner, (dc, 2ch, dc) in next corner 3-ch space; repeat from * around, join with a ss to first dc made. Fasten off.

Afghan square

Size No. 3.00 crochet hook and medium-weight yarn produce a square 8cm across.

Materials and uses Make a brightly coloured rug from oddments of double knitting or chunky yarn, or use machine-washable yarn in pretty pastel shades for a baby blanket.

This square uses 5 colours, A, B, C, D and E.

Using A make 4ch and join into a ring with a ss into first ch.

Round 1 3ch, 2tr into ring, (2ch, 3tr into ring) 3 times, 2ch, join with a ss to 3rd of first 3ch. Break off A.

Round 2 Join in B to any 2ch space, 3ch, 2tr, 2ch, 3tr into 2ch space, (1ch, 3tr, 2ch, 3tr into next 2ch space) 3 times, 1ch, join with a ss to 3rd of first 3ch. Break off B.

Round 3 Join in C to corner 2ch space, 3ch, 2tr, 2ch, 3tr into 2ch space, (1ch, 3tr into next 1ch space, 1ch, 3tr, 2ch, 3tr into next 2ch space) 3 times, 1ch, 3tr into next 1ch space, 1ch, join with a ss to 3rd of first 3ch.

Break off C.

Round 4 Join in D to corner 2ch space, 3ch, 2tr, 2ch, 3tr into 2ch space, *(1 ch, 3tr into next 1ch space) twice, 1ch, 3tr, 2ch, 3tr into next 2ch space; repeat from * 3 more times, (1ch, 3tr into next 1ch space) twice, 1ch, join with a ss to 3rd of first 3ch. Break off D.

Round 5 Join in E to corner 2ch space, 3ch, 2tr, 2ch, 3tr into 2ch space, *(1ch, 3tr into next 1ch space) 3 times, 1ch, 3tr, 2ch, 3tr into next 2ch space; repeat from * 3 more times, (1ch, 3tr into next 1ch space) 3 times, 1ch, join with a ss to 3rd of first 3ch. Fasten off.

HEXAGONS

As with square designs, hexagons can be joined together to create a solid fabric, so they are particularly suitable for warm blankets and rugs. By making use of leftover scraps of yarn a patchwork effect can be achieved with the Tinkerbell *pattern, p.47.*

Ribbed hexagon

Size No. 3.50 crochet hook and crêpe cotton produce a hexagon 9cm across (6 rounds worked).
Materials and uses Make a cushion cover from slub linen or cotton yarn, or use thick cotton for place mats and coasters.

Make 4ch and join into a ring with a ss into first ch.
Round 1 3ch to count as first tr, (1tr, 1ch, 1tr) 5 times into ring, 1tr into ring, 1ch, join with a ss to 3rd of first 3ch (12tr).
Round 2 Ss into first tr and first ch space, 4ch to count as first tr and 1ch space, 1tr into same place as last ss, inserting hook from back to front work 1tr round stem of next tr – called 1tr back –, 1tr back into next tr, *(1tr, 1ch, 1tr) into next 1ch space, 1tr back into each of next 2tr; repeat from * 4 more times, (1tr, 1ch, 1tr) into last 1ch space, 1tr back round first 3ch of round 1, 1tr back round first tr of round 1, join with a ss to 3rd of first 4ch (24tr).
Round 3 Ss into first 1ch space, 4ch to count as first tr and 1ch space, 1tr into same 1ch space, *1tr back into each of next 4tr, (1tr, 1ch, 1tr) into next 1ch space; repeat from * 4 more times, 1tr back into each of next 4 sts, join with a ss to 3rd of first 4ch (36tr). Continue in this way, increasing 12 tr on each round, working 1tr back into each tr on sides and (1tr, 1ch, 1tr) into each 1ch space at corners until hexagon is the required size. Fasten off.

Blue belle

Size No. 2.50 crochet hook and medium-weight wool produce a hexagon 8cm across.

Materials and uses Make a tea cosy from oddments of chunky or double knitting wool, or use lurex and chenille for a novelty cushion.

This design uses 3 colours, A, B and C.

Using A, make 4ch and join into a ring with a ss into first ch.

Round 1 3ch, yarn over hook, insert hook in ring and draw loop out to length of 3-ch, yarn over hook and draw through all 3 loops on hook − a long htr made −, make 16 more long htr in ring, join with a ss to top of 3-ch. Break off A.

Round 2 Join in B, 1ch and, working through the 2 back loops only of each long htr, make dc in each st around, thus forming a ridge on right side (36dc in round), join by inserting hook in first dc made and drawing through a loop of C. Do not break off B.

Round 3 Working over B with C,

make 4ch, 3dtr in base of ch, *drop C (do not work over it) and, with B, yarn over hook twice and, holding back on hook the last loop of each dtr, make dtr in same place as C dtrs and in each of next 6 sts, drop B and, with C, yarn over hook and draw through all 8 loops on hook − a cluster made −, working over B, make 7 C dtr in same place as last B dtr of cluster; repeat from * around, ending with C, 3dtr in same place as last B dtr of cluster, join with a ss to top of 4-ch. Break off B.

Round 4 3ch, tr in next 7 sts, 2ch, 2tr in same place, *tr in next 7 sts, in next st make 2tr, 2ch and 2 tr; repeat from * around, join with a ss to top of 3-ch. Fasten off.

Tinkerbell

Size No. 3.50 crochet hook and medium-weight yarn produce a hexagon 6.5cm across.
Materials and uses Make a baby's blanket from machine-washable medium-weight crêpe, or use chunky yarn for a blanket.

This hexagon uses 4 colours, A, B, C and D.
Using A, make 5ch and join into a ring with a ss into first ch.
Round 1 3ch, 1tr in ring, *1ch, 2tr in ring; repeat from * 4 more times, 1ch, join with a ss to top of ch-3. Break off A.
Round 2 Join in B to first 1-ch space, 3ch, (1tr, 1ch, 2tr) in same space, 1ch, *(2tr, 1ch, 2tr) for shell in next 1-ch space, 1ch; repeat from * 4 more times, join with a ss to top of 3-ch.

Break off B.
Round 3 Join in C to 1-ch space of first shell, 3ch, (1tr, 1ch, 2tr) in same space, *1ch, 2tr in 1-ch space between shells, 1ch, (2tr, 1ch, 2tr) in 1-ch space of next shell; repeat from * 4 times, 1ch, 2tr in next 1-ch space, 1ch, ss in top of 3ch. Break off C.
Round 4 Join in D to 1-ch space of first shell, 1ch, 1dc in each tr and each 1-ch space between shells, 2dc in each 1-ch space of shells, join with a ss to first 1-ch. Fasten off.

Anemone

Size No. 2.50 crochet hook and medium-weight cotton produce a hexagon 7.5cm across.

Materials and uses Make a shawl for special occasions from mohair or angora, or use thick bouclé or terry-mix cotton for a bath mat.

This hexagon uses 4 colours, A, B, C and D.

Using A, make 9ch and join into a ring with a ss into first ch.

Round 1 1ch, 18dc into ring, join with a ss to first dc made. Break off A.

Round 2 Join in B to any dc, 3ch, tr in each of next 2dc, 6ch, *tr in each of next 3dc, 6ch; repeat from * 4 more times, join with a ss to 3rd ch of 3-ch. Break off B.

Round 3 Join in C to first tr of any 3-tr group, 3ch, 2tr in next tr, tr in 3rd tr, 4ch, *in next 3-tr group work tr in first tr, 2tr in second tr, tr in 3rd tr, 4ch; repeat from * 4 more times, join with a ss to 3rd ch of 3-ch. Break off C.

Round 4 Join in D to first tr of any 4-tr group, 3ch, tr in each of next 3tr, 3ch, dc loosely over the 2 chain loops below, 3ch, *tr in each of next 4tr, 3ch, dc loosely over the 2 chain loops below, 3ch; repeat from * 4 more times, join with a ss to third ch of 3-ch. Fasten off.

To join Sew together the 4-tr edges only.

Pinwheel

Size No. 2.50 crochet hook and medium-weight cotton produce a hexagon 6.5cm across.

Materials and uses Create a baby's blanket or pram cover from oddments of medium-weight yarn, or use chunky yarn for a cushion cover.

This hexagon uses 4 colours, A, B, C and D.

Using A, make 5ch and join into a ring with ss into first ch.

Round 1 6ch, (tr in ring, 3ch) 5 times, 3ch, join with a ss to 3rd ch of 6-ch. Break off A.

Round 2 Join in B to any tr, pull up loop on hook to 2cm, *(yrh, insert hook under the tr st and pull through a 2cm loop) 4 times, yrh and through all loops on hook, 1ch tightly, (puff st made), 5ch; repeat from * 5 times, working under every tr st around, including the 3-ch, join with a ss to top of first puff st. Break off B.

Round 3 Join in C to any 5-ch space, 3ch, (2tr, 2ch, 3tr) in same space, *(3tr, 2ch, 3tr) in next space; repeat from * 4 times, join with a ss to 3rd ch of 3-ch. Break off C.

Round 4 Join in D to any 2-ch space, (dc, 2ch, dc) in same space, *dc in every tr till next corner 2-ch space, (dc, 2ch, dc) in 2-ch space; repeat from * 4 times, dc in every remaining st, join with a ss to first dc made. Fasten off.

Ornate hexagon

Size No. 2.50 crochet hook and fine cotton produce a hexagon 9.5cm across.

Materials and uses Use fine cotton for an appliqué motif for a cushion, or make a matching luncheon set from medium-weight cotton.

This hexagon uses 2 colours, A and B. Using A, wind yarn 20 times round one finger, then slip loop off finger. Catch ring together with a ss.

Round 1 4ch, 4dtr into ring, (2ch, 5dtr into ring) 5 times, 2ch, join with a ss to top of 4ch at beginning of round. Break off A.

Round 2 Join in B to any 2ch space, 2dc into same space, (9ch, 2dc into next space) 6 times omitting last 2dc, join with a ss to beginning of round.

Round 3 (1dc into each of next 2dc, 13dc into 9ch loop) 6 times, join with a ss to beginning of round.

Round 4 Ss into each of next 5dc, (1dc into each of next 7dc, 9ch, miss next 8dc) 6 times.

Round 5 *1dc into each dc of next group, (3ch, ss to top of last dc − picot made −, 2dc into 9ch loop) 4 times, 3ch, ss to top of last dc; repeat from * all around. Fasten off.

Spoked hexagon

Size No. 3.00 crochet hook and medium-weight wool produce a hexagon 12cm across (7 rounds worked).

Materials and uses Make cushion covers from medium-weight or double knitting wool, or use cotton crêpe for place mats and coasters.

Make 5ch and join into a ring with a ss into first ch.

Round 1 4ch to count as first tr, and 1ch space, (2ch, 1ch) 5 times into ring, 1tr into ring, join with a ss to 3rd of first 3ch (12tr).

Round 2 3ch to count as first tr, *2tr into next 1ch space, 1tr into next tr, 2ch, 1tr into next tr; repeat from * 4 more times, 1tr into next tr, 2ch, join with a ss to 3rd of first 3ch (24tr).

Round 3 3ch to count as first tr, 1tr at base of 3ch, *1tr into each of next 2tr, 2tr into next tr, 3ch, 2tr into next tr; repeat from * 4 more times, 1tr into each of next 2tr, 2tr into next tr, 3ch, join with a ss to 3rd of first 3ch (36tr).

Round 4 3ch to count as first tr, 1tr at base of 3ch, *1tr into each of next 4tr, 2tr into next tr, 3ch, 2tr into next tr; repeat from * 4 more times, 1tr into each of next 4tr, 2tr into next tr, 3ch, join with a ss to 3rd of first 3ch (48tr).

Continue in this way, increasing 12tr on each round, working 3ch at each corner, until hexagon is the required size. Fasten off.

Little spindles

Size No. 3.00 crochet hook and crêpe cotton produce a hexagon 6.5cm across.

Materials and uses For place mats join together seven hexagons made from medium-weight yarn, or use washable yarn for a pram cover.

Make 6ch and join into a ring with a ss into first ch.

Round 1 5ch, (dtr in ring, 2ch) 11 times, join with a ss to 3rd ch of 5-ch (12 spaces).

Round 2 Ss into next 2-ch space, (3ch, tr, 2ch, 2tr) in same space, 3tr in next space, *(2tr, 2ch, 2tr) in next space, 3tr in next space; repeat from * 4 more times, join with a ss to 3rd ch of 3-ch. Fasten off.

Snowflake

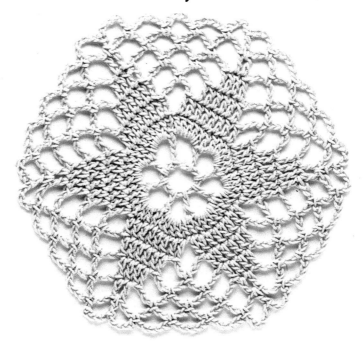

Size No. 2.50 crochet hook and fine cotton produce a hexagon 13cm across.

Materials and uses Make a tablecloth from fine or medium-weight cotton, or make a shawl from fine angora.

Make 12 ch and join into a ring with a ss into first ch.

Round 1 7ch (to count as tr and 4ch), tr in ring, (4ch, tr in ring) 6 times, 4ch, join with a ss to 3rd st of 7ch.

Round 2 3ch (to count as tr), *5 tr in next space, tr in next tr; repeat from * around, join with a ss to top of 3ch.

Round 3 3ch, tr in next 7tr, 5ch, *tr in next 8tr, 5ch; repeat from * around, join (6 groups of tr with 5ch between groups).

Round 4 Ss in next tr, 3ch, tr in next 5tr, *5ch, dc in loop, 5ch, miss 1tr, tr in next 6tr; repeat from * around, end with 5ch, dc in loop, 5ch, join.

Round 5 Ss in next tr, 3ch, tr in next 3tr, *(5ch, dc in next loop) twice, 5ch, miss 1tr, tr in next 4tr; repeat from * around, join.

Round 6 Ss in next tr, 3ch, tr in next tr, *(5ch, dc in next loop) 3 times, 5ch, miss 1tr, tr in next 2tr; repeat from * around, join.

Round 7 Ss between 3ch and tr, 8ch *(dc in next loop, 5ch) 4 times, tr between next 2tr, 5ch; repeat from * around, join last 5ch to 3rd st of 8ch. Fasten off. These hexagons may be crocheted together on the 7th round.

Rounds 1–6 As rounds 1–6 above.

Round 7 Ss between 3ch and tr, 8ch, (dc in next loop, 5ch) 4 times, tr between next 2tr, (2ch, dc in corresponding loop on first hexagon, 2ch, dc in next loop on 2nd hexagon) 4 times, 2ch, dc in next loop on first hexagon, 2ch, tr between next 2tr on 2nd hexagon, complete round as for 1st hexagon.

Subsequent hexagons may be joined in this way along one or more sides.

Rosette

Size No. 2.50 crochet hook and fine cotton produce a motif 5.5cm across.

Materials and uses Join together seven motifs made from different shades of medium-weight cotton for pretty place mats, or use chunky cotton yarn for a bedspread.

This design uses 2 colours, A and B. Using A, make 9ch and join into a ring with a ss into first ch.

Round 1 3ch, 2tr in ring, *6ch, ss sideways in last tr made, 3tr in ring; repeat from * 4 times, 6ch, ss in last tr, ss in 3rd ch of 3-ch. Break off A.

Round 2 Join in B to any centre tr of any 3-tr group, *work 11tr sts into 6-ch loop, ss in centre tr of next 3-tr group; repeat from * 5 more times, ss in st where yarn was attached. Fasten off.

To join Sew top edge stitches of petals together.

Hidden petals

Size No. 2.00 crochet hook and fine cotton produce a hexagon 8cm across.

Materials and uses Make a tablecloth from fine, washable cotton, or use silky yarn to make a luxurious evening shawl.

Make 6ch and join into a ring with a ss into first ch.

Round 1 3ch, 11tr in ring, join with a ss to 3rd ch of 3-ch.

Round 2 3ch, tr in joining, 2tr in next tr, *1ch, 2tr in each of next 2tr; repeat from * 4 times, 1ch, join with a ss to 3rd ch of 3-ch.

Round 3 3ch, tr in joining, tr in each of next 2tr, 2tr in 3rd tr, *2ch, miss 1ch, 2tr in next tr, tr in each of next 2tr, 2tr in next tr; repeat from * 4 times, 2ch, join with a ss to 3rd ch of 3-ch.

Round 4 3ch, tr in joining, tr in each of next 4tr, 2tr in last tr of section, *3ch, 2tr in first tr of next section, tr in each of next 4tr, 2tr in last tr of section; repeat from * 4 times, 3ch, join with a ss to 3rd ch of 3-ch.

Round 5 3ch, tr in joining, tr in each of next 6tr, 2tr in last tr of section, *4ch, 2tr in first tr of next section, tr in each of next 6tr, 2tr in last tr of section; repeat from * 4 times, 4ch, join with a ss to 3rd ch of 3-ch. Fasten off.

To join Arrange hexagons as illustrated and sew tr stitches of adjoining medallions together, not the chain loops.

Flower hexagon

Size No. 3.00 crochet hook and medium-weight cotton produce a hexagon 12cm across (6 rounds worked).

Materials and uses Make place mats and coasters from machine-washable yarn, or use multi-coloured wool for cushion covers.

Make 6ch and join into a ring with a ss into first ch.

Round 1 3ch, leaving last loop of each tr on hook work 2tr into ring, yrh and draw through all 3 loops on hook − called 2tr cluster −, *3ch, leaving last loop of each tr on hook work 3tr into ring, yrh and draw through all 4 loops on hook − called 3tr cluster −; repeat from * 4 more times, 1ch, 1htr into top of 2tr cluster (6 clusters).

Round 2 3ch, 2tr cluster into side of htr just worked, *3ch, (3tr cluster, 3ch, 3tr cluster) into next 3ch loop; repeat from * ending 3ch, 3tr into top of htr on previous round, 1ch, 1htr into 3rd of first 3ch (12 clusters).

Round 3 3ch to count as first tr, 2tr cluster into top of htr just worked, *3ch, (3tr cluster, 3ch, 3tr cluster) into next 3ch loop, 3ch, 3tr cluster into next 3ch loop; repeat from * 4 more times, 3ch, (3tr cluster, 3ch, 3tr cluster) into next 3ch loop, 1ch, 1htr into 3rd of first 3ch (18 clusters).

Round 4 3ch, 1tr into side of htr just worked, 2tr into next 3ch loop, *(2tr, 2ch, 2tr) into next 3ch loop, (2tr into next 3ch loop) twice; repeat from * 4 times, (2tr, 2ch, 2tr) into next 3ch loop, join with ss to 3rd of 1st 3ch.

Round 5 3ch to count as first tr, 1tr into each of next 5tr, *3tr into next 2ch space, 1tr into each of next 8tr; repeat from * 4 times, 3tr into next 2ch space, 1tr into each of next 2tr, join with ss to top of first 3ch (66tr).

Round 6 3ch to count as first tr, 1tr into each of next 6tr, *3tr into next tr, 1tr into each of next 10tr; repeat from * 4 more times, 3tr into next tr, 1tr into each of next 3tr, join with a ss to top of first 3ch (78tr).

Continue in this way, increasing 12tr on each round, working 3tr into each tr at corners, until hexagon is the required size. Fasten off.

Afghan hexagon

Size No. 3.00 crochet hook and medium-weight wool produce a hexagon 12cm across (7 rounds worked).

Materials and uses Use oddments of medium-weight or double knitting wool for a multi-coloured blanket, or make a shawl from silky yarn or wool crêpe.

This hexagon uses 2 colours, A and B.
Using A, make 4ch and join into a ring with a ss into first ch.
Round 1 1ch, 12dc into ring, join with a ss to first ch (12dc).
Round 2 5ch to count as first tr and 2ch space, *(1tr, 2ch) into next dc; repeat from * to end, join with a ss to 3rd of first 5ch (12 2-ch spaces). Break off A.
Round 3 Join in B with a ss into first 2ch space, 3ch, leaving last loop of each tr on hook work 3tr into next 2ch space, yrh and draw through all 4 loops on hook − first cluster worked −, *3ch, leaving last loop of each tr on hook work 4tr into next 2ch space, yrh and draw through all 5 loops on hook; repeat from * ending 3ch, join with a ss to 3rd of first 3ch. Break off B.
Round 4 Join in A with a ss into top of first cluster and first ch of first 3ch loop, 3ch to count as first tr, 3tr into same loop, *1ch, 4 tr into next 3ch loop; repeat from * ending 1ch, join

with a ss to 3rd of first 3ch (48tr). Break off A.
Round 5 Join in B with a ss into first 3tr and 1ch space, 3ch to count as first tr, (2tr, 2ch, 3tr) into first 1ch space, *2ch, 4tr into next 1ch space, 2ch, (3tr, 2ch, 3tr) into next 1ch space; repeat from * 4 more times, 2ch, 4tr into next 1ch space, 2ch, join with a ss to 3rd of first 3ch (1 group of 4tr on each edge). Break off B.
Round 6 Join in A with a ss into first 2tr, 3ch to count as first tr, (2tr, 2ch, 3tr) into first 2ch space, *2ch, (4tr into next 2ch space, 2ch) twice, (3tr, 2ch, 3tr) into next 2ch space; repeat from * 4 more times, 2ch, (4tr into next 2ch space, 2ch) twice, join with a ss to 3rd of first 3ch (2 groups of 4tr on each edge). Break off A.
Continue in this way, increasing 1 group of 4tr on each edge, working (3tr, 2ch, 3tr) into each 2ch space at the corners until hexagon is the required size. Fasten off.

Cobweb

Size No. 3.00 crochet hook and medium-weight yarn produce a design 8cm across.

Materials and uses Use fine silky cotton or mohair glitter yarn to create a luxurious evening shawl, or use chunky cotton for place mats and coasters.

Make 4ch and join into a ring with a ss into first ch.

Round 1 3ch, 17tr in ring, join with a ss to top of 3ch.

Round 2 *5ch, miss 2 sts, 1dc in next st; repeat from * 4 more times, 5ch, 1dc in first st of 5ch.

Round 3 *7ch, 1dc in next dc; repeat from * 4 more times, 7ch, 1dc in first st of 7ch.

Round 4 *9ch, 1dc in next dc; repeat from * 4 more times, 9ch, 1dc in first st of 9ch.

Round 5 *11ch, 1dc in next dc; repeat from * 4 more times, 11ch, 1dc in first st of 11ch.

Round 6 *13ch, 1dc in next dc; repeat from * 4 more times, 13ch, 1dc in first st of 13ch. Fasten off.

TRIANGLES

Triangular motifs can be combined with hexagons to make even more interesting designs, or they can be used on their own. Their shape makes them particularly suitable for making shawls or headscarves, but they can of course be used for virtually any crochet project.

Lace triangle

Size No. 2.50 crochet hook and fine cotton produce a triangle with sides 6cm long.
Materials and uses Join several made from medium-weight yarn for place mats and coasters, or use thick cotton for a bedspread.

This triangle uses 3 colours, A, B and C.
Using A, make 6ch and join into a ring with a ss into first ch.
Round 1 4ch, (tr in ring, 1 ch) 11 times, join with a ss to 3rd ch of 4-ch. Break off A.
Round 2 Join in B to any 1-ch space, 4ch, * (dtr, 7ch, dtr) in next space, (1ch, tr in next space) 3 times, 1ch; repeat from * once more, (dtr, 7ch, dtr) in next space, (1ch, tr in next space) 2 times, 1ch, join with a ss to 3rd ch of 4-ch. Break off B.
Round 3 Join in C to the 1-ch space before any corner dtr, dc in same space, * 1ch, (dc, 1ch, dc, 5ch, dc, 1ch, dc) in corner 7-ch space, (1ch, dc in next 1-ch space) 4 times; repeat from * once more, 1ch, (dc, 1ch, dc, 5ch, dc, 1ch, dc) in next space, (1ch, dc in next 1-ch space) 3 times, 1ch, join with a ss to first dc made.
Fasten off.

Shell triangle

Size No. 4.00 crochet hook and double knitting wool produce a triangle with sides 8.5cm long.
Materials and uses Use up oddments of brightly coloured

double knitting yarn to make a cushion cover, or make a bedspread from chunky wool.

This triangle uses 3 colours, A, B and C.
Using A, make 4ch and join into a ring with a ss into first ch.
Round 1 3ch to count as 1tr, 11tr into ring, join with a ss into top of 3ch.
Round 2 (5ch, ss into 4th tr of previous round) twice, 5ch, join with ss. Break off A.
Round 3 Join in B into first 5ch space, 3ch to count as 1tr, 6tr, 2ch, (7tr 2ch) twice, join to top of 3ch. Break off B.
Round 4 Join in C to any 2ch space, 3ch, 8tr into 2ch space, 7dc, (9tr into 2ch space, 7dc) twice, ss into top of first 3ch. Fasten off.

Eternal triangle

Size No. 3.00 crochet hook and medium-weight yarn produce a triangle with sides 9cm long.
Materials and uses Make potholders from leftover double knitting or chunky yarn, or use chunky cotton for coasters.

Make 4ch and join into a ring with a ss into first ch.
Round 1 3ch to count as 1tr, 11tr into ring, join with a ss into 3rd of first 3ch.
Round 2 (5ch, ss into 4th tr of previous round) twice, 5ch, join with a ss to base of first 5ch.
Round 3 Ss into 5ch sp, 3ch to count as 1tr, 6tr, 2ch, (7tr, 2ch) twice, join to top of 3ch.
Round 4 2ch, 6htr, 9tr in 2ch sp, (7htr, 9tr in 2ch sp) twice, ss in top of 2ch.
Round 5 4ch, (miss htr, 1tr, 1ch,) 5 times, *1tr, in next tr, 4ch, miss 1tr, 1tr in next tr, 1ch, 1tr, (1ch, miss 1tr, 1tr), 6 times, 1ch, repeat from * once more, 1tr, 4ch, miss 1tr, 1tr, 1ch, 1tr, 1ch, ss in 3rd ch at start.
Round 6 3ch, 1tr in 1ch sp, 1tr in each tr to 4ch sp, 3tr, 2ch, 3tr, into corner sp, all round, ss in top of 3ch. Fasten off.

Crossed triangle

Size No. 3.00 crochet hook and medium-weight cotton produce a triangle with sides 17cm long.

Materials and uses Join together two large triangles made from chunky yarn for a novelty cushion cover, or make coasters from medium-weight cotton.

Make 6ch and join into a ring with a ss into first ch.

Round 1 2ch, *into ring work 3tr but keep last loop of each tr on hook, then draw a loop through all loops on hook – called 1 cluster –, 5ch; repeat from * twice more.

Round 2 *1dc into cluster, 3ch, (3tr, 3ch, 3tr, 3ch) into ch loop of previous round; repeat from * twice more.

Round 3 1dc into ch loop, 3ch, (3tr, 3ch, 3tr, 3ch) into ch loop between 3tr groups, (1dc, 3ch) into next 2ch loops; repeat from * twice more.

Round 4 *1tr into each tr, (2tr, 3ch, 2tr) into ch loop, 1tr into each tr, 3ch, 1tr into next ch loop, 1 cluster into next ch loop, 1tr into next ch loop, 3ch; repeat from * twice more.

Round 5 *1tr into each tr (2tr, 3ch, 2tr) into ch loop, 1tr into each tr, 3ch, 1dc into next ch loop, 3ch, 1dc into next ch loop, 3ch; repeat from * twice more.

Round 6 As round 4.

Round 7 As round 5.

Round 8 * 1 dc into each tr, 3dc into corner ch loop, 1dc into each tr, (1dc into ch loop) 3 times; repeat from * twice more, join with a ss, work 1 ch then work another row of dc right round, but working from left to right instead of from right to left. Fasten off.

Tricorn

Size No. 4.00 crochet hook and double knitting yarn produce a triangle with sides 9cm long.

Materials and uses Use oddments of chunky yarn in bright colours for a blanket, or use subtle shades of medium-weight cotton for a cushion cover.

This triangle uses 4 colours, A, B, C and D.

Using A, make 4ch and join into a ring with a ss into first ch.

Round 1 3ch, 11tr in ring, join with a ss to 3rd ch of 3-ch. Break off A.

Round 2 Join in B to any tr, 3ch, 4tr in same st, *htr in next st, dc in next st, tr in next st, 5tr in 4th st; repeat from * once more, htr, dc, tr, join with a ss to 3rd ch of 3-ch. Break off B.

Round 3 Join in C to 3rd tr of any 5-tr corner, 3ch, 4tr in same st, *htr in each of next 7 sts, 5tr in 8th st; repeat from * around, join with a ss to 3rd ch of 3-ch. Break off C.

Round 4 Join in D to middle tr of any 5-tr corner, 1ch, (2dc, 1ch, 2dc) in same st, *dc in every st till next corner's middle tr st, (2dc, 1ch, 2dc) in that st; repeat from * around, join with a ss to first dc made. Fasten off.

CIRCLES & OCTAGONS

When circular or octagonal designs are joined together, there will be spaces between the various elements. These spaces may be filled with small filler motifs (see pp. 79–84), or they may be left as they are to create a delicate, lacy fabric.
Many of the more solid designs in this chapter can easily be made into cushions by working more rounds until the medallion is the required size.

Plain circle

Size No. 4.00 crochet hook and cotton crêpe produce a circle 12.5cm across (5 rounds worked).
Materials and uses Make cushions from double knitting or chunky yarn, or use medium-weight or crêpe cotton for place mats and coasters.

Make 3ch and join into a ring with a ss into first ch.
Round 1 3ch, 15tr into ring, join with a ss into top of first ch.
Round 2 3ch, 2tr into each tr to end, join with a ss into top of first ch.
Round 3 3ch, *2tr into next tr, 1tr; repeat from * around, join with a ss into first ch.
Round 4 3ch, *tr into first tr, 2tr, repeat from * around, join with a ss into first ch.
Round 5 3ch, *tr into first tr, 3tr, repeat from * around, join with a ss into first ch. Fasten off.

Lemon and lime

Size No. 3.50 crochet hook and medium-weight wool produce an octagon 7.5cm across.

Material and uses Use oddments of chunky yarn for a blanket.

This octagon uses 3 colours A, B and C.

Using A, Make 5ch and join into a ring with a ss into first ch.

Round 1 4ch, 15tr in ring, join with a ss to top of 4ch.

Round 2 5ch, *1tr in back loop only of next st, 2ch; repeat from * to end of round, join with a ss to 3rd st of 5ch. Break off A.

Round 3 Join in B to any tr, 3ch, *2tr in next 2ch space, 1tr in next tr, 4ch, 1tr in next tr; repeat from * 6 more times, 2tr in next 2ch space, 1tr in next tr, 4ch, join with a ss to top of first 3ch. Break off B.

Round 4 Join in C to ss, 1ch, working into back loops only, 1htr in each st of previous round. Fasten off.

Peach sorbet

Size No. 3.50 crochet hook and medium-weight wool produce an octagon 7cm across.

Materials and uses Make a pram cover from acrylic yarn, or use chunky wool for a tea cosy.

This octagon uses 2 colours, A and B.

Using A make 6ch and join into a ring with a ss into first ch.

Round 1 2ch, 23tr in ring, join with a ss to top of 2ch.

Round 2 4ch, 1tr in same st, 1ch, *miss 2 sts, (1tr, 2ch, 1tr) in next st, 1ch; repeat from * 6 more times, join with a ss to 2nd st of 4ch. Break off A.

Round 3 Join in B, 2ch, (1tr, 2ch 2tr) in first 2ch space, *1tr in 1ch space, (2tr, 2ch, 2tr) in next 2ch space; repeat from * 6 more times, 1tr in last 1ch space, join with a ss to top of 2ch.

Round 4 1dc in each st, 2dc in each 2ch space to end of round, join with a ss to first dc. Fasten off.

Catherine wheel

Size No. 2.50 crochet hook and lurex yarn produce a design 10cm across.

Materials and uses Make an appliqué motif for a cushion from fine cotton, or use medium-weight cotton for coasters.

Wind yarn 20 times round one finger, then slip loop off finger. Catch ring together with a ss. **Round 1** Work 21dc into ring, join with a ss to first dc. **1st "arm"** 10ch, fasten a safety-pin to 10th ch, work 20dc back over 10ch, ss into next dc of round 1, turn, (4ch, miss 4dc, 1dc into next dc) 4 times, turn, (6dc into next 4ch loop) 4 times, miss next dc on round 1, join with a ss to following dc, turn. **2nd "arm"** 10ch, ss to centre dc of 2nd loop from centre, turn, work 20 dc into 10ch loop, ss into next dc of round 1, complete "arm" as before. Work 5 more "arms" and join last to the first with a ss into place marked with a safety-pin, working (3dc, ss, 3dc) into 3rd 4ch loop instead of 6dc, 6dc into 4th 4ch loop, ss into last dc in ring. Fasten off.

Striped octagon

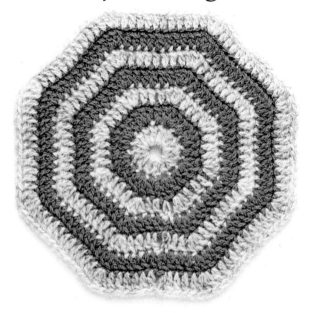

Size No. 3.50 crochet hook and medium-weight wool produce an octagon 14.5cm across (7 rounds worked).

Materials and uses Make a blanket from oddments of double knitting or chunky yarn, or use novelty yarn or bouclé for a cushion cover.

This octagon uses 2 colours, A and B. Using A, make 5ch and join into a ring with a ss into first ch.

Round 1 3ch to count as first tr, 15tr into ring, join with a ss to 3rd of first 3ch (16 sts). Break off A.

Round 2 Join in B, 3ch to count as first tr, 2tr at base of 3ch, *1tr into next tr, 3tr into next tr; repeat from * 6 more times, 1tr into next tr, join with a ss to 3rd of first 3ch (32sts). Break off B.

Round 3 Join in A, 3ch to count as first tr, *3tr into next tr, 1tr into each of next 3tr; repeat from * 6 more times, 3tr into next tr, 1tr into each of next 2tr, join with a ss to 3rd of first 3ch (48 sts). Break off A.

Round 4 Join in B, 3ch to count as first tr, 1tr into next tr, *3tr into next tr, 1tr into each of next 5tr; repeat from * 6 more times, 3tr into next tr, 1tr into each of next 3tr, join with a ss to 3rd of first 3ch (64sts). Break off B.

Continue in this way, increasing 16 sts on each round, working 3tr into tr at each corner, and changing colour every round, until octagon is the required size. Fasten off.

Filet octagon

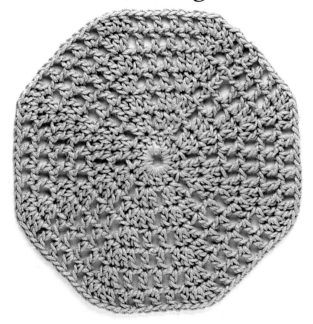

Size No. 3.50 crochet hook and crêpe cotton produce an octagon 15cm across (7 rounds worked).
Materials and uses Use medium-weight cotton for place mats and coasters, or make a cushion cover from chunky yarn.

Make 6ch and join into a ring with a ss into first ch.
Round 1 3ch, 15tr into ring, join with a ss to 3rd of first 3ch (16sts).
Round 2 3ch to count as first tr, 2tr into base of 3ch, *1ch, miss next tr, 3tr into next tr; repeat from * 6 more times, 1ch, miss next tr, join with a ss to 3rd of first 3ch (8 1-ch spaces).
Round 3 3ch to count as first tr, *3tr into next tr, 1tr into next tr, 1ch, 1tr into next tr; repeat from * 6 more times, 3tr into next tr, 1tr into next tr, 1ch, join with a ss to 3rd of first 3ch.
Round 4 4ch to count as first tr and 1ch space, miss next tr, *3tr into next tr, 1ch, miss next tr, 1tr into next tr, 1ch, 1tr into next tr, 1ch, miss next tr; repeat from * 6 more times, 3tr into next tr, 1ch, miss next tr, 1ch, join with a ss to 3rd of first 4ch (24

1-ch spaces).
Round 5 4ch to count as first tr and 1ch space, 1tr into next tr, *3tr into next tr, (1tr into next tr, 1ch) 3 times, 1tr into next tr; repeat from * 6 more times, 3tr into next tr, (1tr into next tr, 1ch) twice, join with a ss to 3rd of first 3ch.
Round 6 4ch to count as first tr and 1ch space, 1tr into next tr, 1ch, miss next tr, *3tr into next tr, 1ch, miss next tr, (1tr into next tr, 1ch) 4 times, miss next tr; repeat from * 6 more times, 3tr into next tr, 1ch, miss next tr, (1tr into next tr, 1ch) twice, join with a ss to 3rd of first 4ch (40 1-ch spaces).
Continue in this way, increasing 16 1-ch spaces on every alternate round, working 3tr into tr at each corner until octagon is the required size. Fasten off.

Butterfly wings

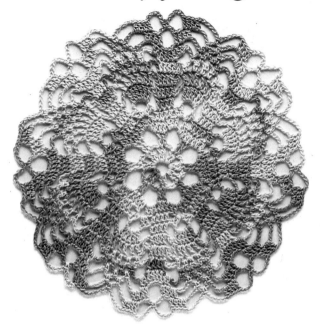

Size No. 1.25 crochet hook and very fine cotton produce a circle 13cm across.

Materials and uses Use very fine cotton for coasters or glass mats.

Make 10ch and join into a ring with a ss into first ch.

Round 1 3ch, tr in ring, (3ch, 2tr in ring) 7 times, 3ch, join with a ss to 3rd st of 3ch.

Round 2 3ch, tr in next tr, (5ch, tr in next 2tr) 7 times, 5ch, join.

Round 3 3ch, tr in next tr, *in next space make 3tr, 2ch and 3tr, tr in next 2tr; repeat from * around, join.

Round 4 3ch, tr in next 2tr, *in next space make 2tr, 5ch and 2tr, miss 2tr, tr in next 4tr; repeat from * around, join.

Round 5 3ch, tr in next 2tr, *3ch, 6dtr in next space, 3ch, miss 2tr, tr in next 4tr; repeat from * around, join.

Round 6 3ch, tr in next 2tr, *4ch, (tr in next dtr, 2ch) 5 times, tr in next dtr, 4ch, tr in next 4tr; repeat from * around, join.

Round 7 3ch, tr in next 2tr, *5ch, miss next space, dc in next space, (3ch, dc in next space) 4 times, 5ch,

miss next space, tr in next 4tr; repeat from * around, join.

Round 8 3ch, tr in next 2tr, *6ch, dc in next 3ch loop, (3ch, dc in next loop) 3 times, 6ch, tr in next 4tr; repeat from * around, join.

Round 9 3ch, tr in next 2tr, 2tr in next space, *6ch, dc in next loop, (3ch, dc in next loop) twice, 6ch, 2tr in space, tr in next 4tr, 2tr in next space; repeat from * around, join.

Round 10 Ss in next 3tr, 3ch, tr in next tr, 2tr in next space, *6ch, dc in next loop, 3ch, dc in next loop, 6ch, 2tr in next space, tr in next 2tr, 4ch, miss 4tr, tr in next 2tr, 2tr in next space; repeat from * around, join.

Round 11 Ss in next 2tr, 3ch, tr in next tr, 2tr in next space, *6ch, dc in next loop, 6ch, 2tr in next space, tr in next 2tr, 6ch, dc in next space, 6ch, miss 2tr, tr in next 2tr, 2tr in next space; repeat from * around, join. Fasten off.

Spinning wheel

Size No. 3.50 crochet hook and medium-weight wool produce a circle 9cm across.

Materials and uses Make a bedspread from medium-weight or double knitting yarn, or use fine cotton for a lacy shawl.

Note *Picot (pc): 3ch, 1htr in top of last htr.*

Make 6ch and join into a ring with a ss into first ch.

Round 1 5ch (1dtr, 2ch in ring) 11 times, join with a ss to 3rd ch.

Round 2 1dc in first 3ch space, 2ch, 2dtr, leaving last loop of each dtr on hook, yrh and draw through 3 loops, 3ch, in each ch space *3dtr leaving last loop of each dtr on hook, yrh and draw through 4 loops − 1 cluster made −, 3ch; repeat from * 10 more times, join with a ss to top of first st.

Round 3 (3htr, 1pc, 2htr) in each space, join with a ss to top of first st. After joining the circles together, the spaces between them may be filled with filler motifs.

Filler motif
Note *Picot (pc): 3ch, 1htr in top of last dc.*

Make 6ch and join into a ring with a ss into first ch.

Round 1 3ch, 1htr in ss, *1dc, 1tr, 1dtr, 1tr tr, 1dtr, 1tr, 1dc, 1pc; repeat from * 2 more times, 1dc, 1tr, 1dtr, 1tr tr, 1dtr, 1tr, 1dc, join with a ss to top of first ch. Fasten off.

Scallops and circles

Size No. 1.25 crochet hook and very fine cotton produce a circle 18.5cm across.

Materials and uses Make doilies or place mats from fine cotton.

Make 8ch and join into a ring with a ss into first ch.

Round 1 1ch, 12dc in ring, join with a ss to first dc.

Round 2 4ch, *tr in next dc, 1ch; repeat from * around, joining last 1ch with a ss in 3rd st of starting chain.

Round 3 6ch, tr in same places as ss, *in next tr make tr, 3ch and tr; repeat from * around, join with a ss to 3rd st of starting chain.

Round 4 1ch, make 5dc in each 3-ch space around, join.

Round 5 7ch, *miss next dc, dtr in next dc, 3ch; repeat from * around, join with a ss to 4th st of starting chain.

Round 6 4ch, dtr in next dtr, *5ch, holding back on hook the last loop of each dtr make dtr in same place as last dtr, dtr in next dtr, yarn over and draw through all loops on hook (a joined dtr made); repeat from * around, join.

Round 7 Make 5dc in each 5-ch space around, join.

Round 8 Ss in next 2dc, 9ch, *miss 4dc, dtr in next dc, 5ch; repeat from * around, joining last 5-ch with a ss in 4th st of starting chain.

Round 9 As round 6, having 7-ch spaces instead of 5-ch spaces.

Round 10 Make 9dc in each 7-ch space around, join.

Round 11 Ss in next 4dc, 4ch, 2-dtr cl in same place as last ss, *5ch, 2-dtr cl in 5th ch from hook, miss 8dc, 3-dtr cl in next dc; rep from * around, join.

Round 12 4ch, 2-dtr cl in same place as ss, *6ch, 2-dtr cl in 5th ch from hook, 1ch, 3dtr cl in top of next 3-dtr cl; rep from * around, join.

Round 13 1ch, dc in same place as ss, *11ch, dc in top of next 3-dtr cluster; repeat from * around, join.

Round 14 Work 13dc in each space around, join. Fasten off.

Ruby wine

Size No. 1.25 crochet hook and very fine cotton produce a circle 14cm across.

Materials and uses Use very fine cotton for glass mats, or use any fine yarn for a cushion appliqué motif.

Wind yarn 10 times round one finger, then slip loop off finger.

Round 1 32dc in ring, join with a ss to first dc made.

Round 2 5ch, miss 1dc, tr in next dc, *2ch, miss 1dc, tr in next dc; repeat from * around, ending with 2ch, join with a ss to 3rd st of 5-ch.

Round 3 *10ch, dc in 2nd ch from hook, htr in next ch, tr in next 7ch, dc in next tr of round 2 (a spoke made); repeat from * around ending with dc at base of 10-ch first made (16 spokes in all).

Round 4 Ss to tip of first spoke, 1ch, dc in tip of same spoke, *7ch, dc in tip of next spoke; repeat from *

around, ending with ss in first dc made.

Round 5 5ch, tr in same place as ss, *3ch, dc in next space, 3ch, in next dc make tr, 2ch and tr (shell made); repeat from * around, ending with 3ch, join with a ss to 3rd st of ch-5.

Round 6 Ss in space, 5ch, tr in same space, *4ch, dc in next dc, 4ch, make a shell in space of next shell; repeat from * around ending with 4ch, join with a ss to 3rd st of 5-ch first made.

Rounds 7–9 As round 6, making shell over shell and dc over dc, having 1 additional st in chs between dcs and shells on each successive round. Fasten off.

Prairie rose

Size No. 2.50 crochet hook and fine cotton produce a circle 15cm across.

Materials and uses Make a bedspread from fine cotton, or use very fine cotton for a motif to be applied to a round cushion.

Make 10ch and join into a ring with a ss into first ch.

Round 1 1ch, (dc in ring, 5ch) 6 times, join with a ss to first dc made (6 spaces).

Round 2 In each loop make dc, htr, 5tr, htr and dc (6 petals).

Round 3 *5ch, insert hook in next loop (from back of work) and in following loop (from front of work), yarn over and draw loop through, yarn over and draw through both loops on hook; repeat from * around (6 loops).

Round 4 Work petals as before, making 7 tr (instead of 5) in each petal.

Round 5 Ss in first 3 sts of next petal, dc in next st, *5ch, dc in 3rd ch from hook − picot made −, 3ch, picot, 2ch, miss 3 sts, dc in next st, 2ch, picot, 3ch, picot, 2ch, miss 3 sts of next petal, dc in next st; repeat from * around, join with a ss to first dc made.

Round 6 Ss across to the ch following next picot, ss in loop, 4ch, holding back on hook the last loop of each dtr, make 3dtr in same loop, yarn over and draw through all loops on hook − cluster made −, 3ch, picot, 5ch, picot, 3ch, make a 4-dtr cluster in same loop, in each loop around make cluster, 3ch, picot, 5ch, picot, 3ch and a cluster, join last cluster to top of first cluster. Fasten off.

English rose

Size No. 3.00 crochet hook and medium-weight cotton produce an octagon 18cm across.
Materials and uses Use medium-weight cotton or silky yarn for a bedspread.

Make 10ch and join into a ring with a ss into first ch.
Round 1 1ch, 18dc in ring, join with a ss to first dc made.
Round 2 1ch, dc in same place as ss, *5ch, miss 2dc, dc in next dc; repeat from * 5 more times, 5ch, join with a ss to first dc.
Round 3 1ch, in each loop around make dc, htr, 5tr, htr and dc (6 petals), join.
Round 4 1ch, dc in same place as ss, *7ch, insert hook in next loop from back to front of work, bring it out in next loop from front to back of work, yarn over, draw loop through, yarn over and draw through all loops on hook; repeat from * around, join (6 loops).
Round 5 In each loop around make dc, htr, tr, 7dtr, tr, htr and dc (6 petals).

Round 6 As round 4.
Round 7 Ss in first loop, 3ch, 7tr in same loop, 8tr in each loop around (48tr on round), join with a ss to 3rd st of 3-ch.
Round 8 3ch, tr in next 2tr, *2ch, tr in next 3tr, 4ch, dc in 4th ch from hook – picot made –, tr in next 3tr; repeat from * around, join.
Round 9 3ch, tr in next 2tr, *2ch, tr in next 3tr, 1ch, picot, 1ch, tr in next 3tr; repeat from * around, join.
Round 10 3ch, tr in next 2tr, *2ch, tr in next 3tr, 2ch, picot, 2ch, tr in next 3tr; repeat from * around, join.
Round 11 3ch, tr in next 2tr, *2ch, tr in next 3tr, 11ch, tr in next 3tr; repeat from * around, join.
Round 12 3ch, tr in next 2tr, *2ch, tr in next 3tr, 11tr in next space, tr in next 3tr; repeat from * around, join. Fasten off.

Golden wheel

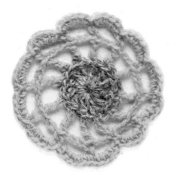

Size No. 3.50 crochet hook and medium-weight wool produce a circle 8cm across.

Materials and uses Use medium-weight or double knitting glitter yarn for coasters, or use silky cotton for a bedspread.

This circle uses 2 colours, A and B. Using A, make 5ch and join into a ring with a ss into first ch.

Round 1 5ch, (1dtr, 1ch) 11 times in ring, ss in 4th st of 5ch. Break off A.

Round 2 Join in B to any tr, 7ch, miss 1ch, (1dtr in back loop only of next st, 3ch, miss 1ch) 11 times, join with a ss to 4th st of 7ch (48sts in round).

Round 3 (4ch, miss 3ch, 1dc in back loop only of next st) 12 times, ending with ss in first st of 4ch.

Round 4 (5htr in 4ch space, ss in next dc) 12 times. Fasten off.

Satellite

Size No. 2.50 crochet hook and fine cotton produce a design 6.5cm across.

Materials and uses Use fine cotton for tablecloth insertion and border, or use medium-weight cotton for place mats.

Make 5ch and join into a ring with a ss into first ch.

Round 1 1ch, 8dc into ring, join with a ss to first dc made.

Round 2 5ch, *tr in next dc, 2ch; repeat from * until 7 spaces are made, 2ch, ss to 3rd ch of 5-ch, (8 spaces).

Round 3 1ch, dc in joining st, *3dc in 2-ch space, dc in tr; repeat from * around, join with a ss to first dc made.

Round 4 1ch, dc in same space, *7ch, miss 3dc, dc in next st; repeat from * around, join with a ss to first dc (8 loops).

Round 5 *Work 9dc in loop, ss in dc; repeat from * around, join with a ss to last dc. Fasten off.

Floral ring

Size No. 3.00 crochet hook and medium-weight cotton produce a circle 12.5cm across.
Materials and uses Make an appliqué motif for a cushion cover from medium-weight cotton or fine multi-coloured cotton.

Wind yarn 20 times round one finger, then slip loop off finger. Catch ring together with a ss.
Round 1 4ch, 4dtr into ring, (2ch, 5dtr into ring) 5 times, 2ch, join with a ss to top of first 4ch.
Round 2 4ch, leaving last loop of each st on hook work 4dtr over next 4dtr, yrh and through all loops on hook – called 4dtr cluster –, (6ch, 1tr into next 2ch space, 6ch, leaving last loop of each st on hook work 5dtr over next 5dtr, yrh and through all loops on hook – called 5dtr cluster) 5 times, 6ch, 1tr into next 2ch space, 6ch, join with a ss to top of first cluster.

Round 3 Ss to centre of next 6ch, 2dc into same loop, *7ch, 2dc into centre of next 6ch loop; repeat from * all round, join with a ss to first dc.
Round 4 Ss into next 7ch loop, 3ch, leaving last loop of each st on hook work 3tr into same loop, yrh and through all loops on hook – called 3tr cluster –, *9ch, leaving last loop of each st on hook work 4tr into same loop, yrh and through all loops on hook – called 4tr cluster –, 4tr cluster into next loop; repeat from * all round, ending with 9ch, 4tr cluster into last loop, join with a ss to top of first cluster. Fasten off.

Sunburst

Size No. 3.50 crochet hook and cotton bouclé produce a circle 19cm across.

Materials and uses Make coasters from multi-coloured cotton, or use thick yarn for plant pot holders.

This circle uses 2 colours, A and B.

Round 1 Using A, 4ch, 11tr in 4th ch from hook, join with a ss to top st of starting chain.

Round 2 Drop A, join in B, 1ch, dc in same place as ss, *2dc in next st, dc in next st; repeat from * around, join with a ss (18sts).

Round 3 Drop B, pick up A, 3ch; 1tr in next st, 2tr in following st to end, join with a ss (32sts).

Round 4 Drop A, pick up B, 1ch; 5dc, 2dc in next st to last 3sts, 3dc, join with a ss (38sts).

Rounds 5 and 6 As rounds 3 and 4, increasing to 52sts and 60sts.

Round 7 As round 3, increasing to 76sts (3tr, 2tr in next st).

Top edging

Round 1 Drop A, pick up B, 1ch, turn and make dc in back loop of each st around, join.

Round 2 Drop B, pick up A, 1ch, dc in same place as ss, *5ch, 3tr where last dc was made, 3dc, dc in next dc; rep from * around, join. Break off A.

Round 3 Pick up B, *5dc in 5-ch loop, dc in next 3tr; repeat from * around. Join and fasten off.

Bottom edging

Join in B and work in remaining free loops of last tr-round of bottom.

Round 1 Dc in each st around, increasing 7dc evenly around (87sts), join.

Round 2 As round 2 of Top edging, 2dc instead of 3sts, join and fasten off. Complete as for Top edging.

Wheel lace

Size No. 1.25 crochet hook and very fine cotton produce a circle 6.5cm across.

Materials and uses Use fine cotton for place mats or a tablecloth, or use medium-weight cotton for a bedspread.

Make 10ch and join into a ring with a ss into first ch.

Round 1 3ch, 23tr in ring, join with a ss to top st of 3-ch.

Round 2 4ch, *tr in next tr, 1ch; repeat from * around, join.

Round 3 Ss in next space, 10ch, *miss 1 space, dtr in next space, 6ch; repeat from * around, join last 6-ch with a ss to 4th st of 10-ch.

Round 4 1ch, dc in same place as ss, *2ch, miss 2ch, tr in next ch, 2ch, tr in next ch, 2ch, dc in next dtr; repeat from * around, join.

Round 5 1ch, dc in same place as ss, *2ch, tr in next tr, 2ch, tr in 2-ch space, 2ch, tr in next tr, 2ch, dc in next dc; repeat from * around, join. Fasten off.

Subsequent circles may be joined together on the 5th round.

Rounds 1 – 4 As rounds 1 – 4 above.

Round 5 1ch, dc in same place as ss, 2ch, tr in next tr, *1ch, ss in corresponding space on first circle, 1ch, tr in next space on 2nd circle, 1ch, ss in next space on first circle, 1ch, tr in next tr on 2nd circle, 2ch, dc in next dc, 2ch, tr in next tr; repeat from * once more, complete round as for first circle.

Ridged octagon

Size No. 3.50 crochet hook and medium-weight yarn produce an octagon 8.5cm across.
Materials and uses Make a shawl from medium-weight glitter yarn, or use flecked wool or novelty yarn for cushion covers.

Make 5ch and join into a ring with a ss into first ch.
Round 1 5ch, (1tr in ring, 2ch) 7 times, join with a ss to 3rd of 5ch.
Round 2 Ss in 2ch space, 3ch, 4tr in same space, 1ch (5tr in next space, 1ch) 7 times, join with a ss to 3rd ch.
Round 3 3ch *2tr in next tr, yrh twice, (bring hook to front of work and inserting hook from right to left, work a dtr through bar of next tr) — called dtr front, 2tr in next tr, 1tr in next tr, 1ch, 1tr in next tr, rep from * 8 times, omitting 1tr in next tr at end of last repeat, join with a ss to 3rd ch.
Round 4 1dc in same st as ss (1htr in next tr, 1tr in next tr, 1dtr front in dtr front, 1htr in next tr, 1dc in next tr, 1ss in 1ch space, 1dc in next tr) 8 times, omitting 1dc in next tr at end of last repeat, join with a ss to first dc. Fasten off.
These octagons may be crocheted together on the 4th round.
Rounds 1–3 As rounds 1–3 above.

Round 4 1dc in same st as ss, 1htr in next tr, 1tr in next tr, 1dtr front in dtr front, ss to top of a dtr front of first octagon, 1tr in next tr on 2nd octagon, 1htr in next tr, 1dc in next tr, 1ss in 1ch space, 1dc in next tr, 1htr in next tr, 1tr in next tr, 1dtr front in next dtr front, ss to top of adjacent dtr front of first octagon, complete round as for first octagon. Subsequent octagons may be joined in this way along one, or more sides. The spaces between the octagons may be filled with filler motifs.

Filler motif
Make 5ch and join into a ring with a ss into first ch.
Round 1 3ch, 3tr in ring, ss in space between 2 petals of octagon (4tr in ring of filler motif, ss between 2 petals of adjacent octagon) twice, 4tr in ring of filler motif, ss between 2 petals of remaining octagon, join with a ss to 3rd of 3ch. Fasten off.

FILLERS & MOTIFS

The small motifs in this chapter are particularly useful for filling in spaces left when octagons or circles are joined together. Use the same colour and type of yarn, or, for more unusual designs, vary the texture and shade. Alternatively these designs can be used as elements themselves, and joined together. Another way of using them is to incorporate them into a simple net background, or use rows of them as very pretty borders.

Starfish

Size No. 3.00 crochet hook and medium-weight cotton produce a motif 8.5cm across.

Materials and uses Make a matching luncheon set from medium-weight cotton: use single motifs for coasters or glass mats, join seven together for place mats, use fine cotton for tiny motifs to attach to fabric serviette holders.

Make 5ch and join into a ring with a ss into first ch.
Round 1 2ch, 11htr in ring, ss in top of 2ch.
Round 2 *7ch, 1htr in 2nd ch from hook, 1htr in each of next 4ch, ss in bottom of ch, ss in back loop only of next 2 sts; repeat from * 5 more times.
Round 3 *1dc in each ch of petal, 5dc in turning ch at top of petal, 1 dc in each htr along other side of petal, ss in st between petals; repeat from * around each petal, ending with ss in st between last and first petal.
Fasten off.

Daisy chain

Size No. 1.25 crochet hook and very fine cotton produce a motif 4cm across.

Materials and uses Make tiny motifs from fine silky or lurex yarn to scatter over an evening shawl, or use cotton crêpe for random appliqué motifs on cushions.

Make 10ch and join into a ring with a ss into first ch.
Round 1 1ch, 18dc in ring, join with a ss to first dc made.
Round 2 4ch (to count as dtr), holding back on hook the last loop of each dtr make 2dtr in same place as ss, yarn over and draw through all loops on hook — 3dtr cluster made —, *10ch, miss 2dc, 3dtr cluster in next dc; repeat from * around, joining last 10ch with a ss in top of first cluster made.
Round 3 * In next loop make 3dc, (3ch, 3dc) 3 times; repeat from * around. Fasten off.

Cactus flower

Size No. 2.50 crochet hook and fine cotton produce a motif 4cm across.

Materials and uses Use pale shades of very fine cotton for scatter appliqué motifs on a christening gown, or use thick cotton yarn and join several together for table mats.

Make 5ch and join into a ring with a ss into first ch.

Round 1 1ch, * dc in ring, 6ch, dc in 2nd ch from hook, htr in next 4ch, dc in ring, 4ch, dc in 2nd ch from hook, htr in next 2ch; repeat from * 3 more times, forming 8 petals, ss in first dc made. Fasten off.

To join Sew tips of petals together.

Tumbleweed

Size No. 2.00 crochet hook and fine cotton produce a motif 5cm across.

Materials and uses Use fine cotton for appliqué motifs round the hem of a little girl's dress, or use as fillers between circles and octagons.

Make 4ch and join into a ring with a ss into first ch.

Round 1 3ch to count as first tr, 11tr into ring, join with a ss to 3rd of first 3ch.

Round 2 * 6ch, ss into 3rd ch from hook to form picot, 4ch, ss into next tr, repeat from * to end, working the last ss into the ss at the end of the first round. Fasten off.

Big wheel

Size No. 2.50 crochet hook and fine cotton produce a motif 6cm across.

Materials and uses Make coasters or glass mats from chunky cotton yarn, or use as a filler motif on larger projects composed of circles or octagons.

Make 7ch and join into a ring with a ss into first ch.

Round 1 3ch, 15tr in ring, join with a ss to top st of ch-3.

Round 2 7ch, *miss 1tr, tr in next tr, 4ch; repeat from * around, joining last 4-ch with ss in 3rd st of 7-ch (8 spaces).

Round 3 Ss in space, 3ch, 7tr in same space, 8tr in each following space around, join and fasten off.

Green florette

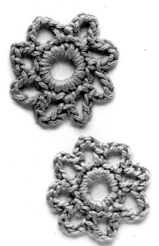

Size No. 3.00 crochet hook and medium-weight cotton produce a motif 4cm across.

Materials and uses Decorate cushion covers with motifs made from silky cotton yarn, or use as a filler on larger projects made from circles or octagons.

Make 8ch and join into a ring with a ss into first ch.

Round 1 1ch, 16dc in ring, join with a ss to first dc made.

Round 2 1ch, dc in same place as ss, *5ch, miss 1dc, dc in next dc; repeat from * around, joining last 5-ch to first dc made. Fasten off.

Powder blue

Size No. 2.50 crochet hook and fine cotton produce a motif 5.5cm across.

Materials and uses Use very fine cotton or silk for scatter appliqué motifs on a wedding dress or christening gown, or decorate the edge of a tablecloth or tray cloth with a row of flowers.

Make 8ch and join into a ring with a ss into first ch.

Round 1 3ch, 2tr in ring, (5ch, dc in 3rd ch from hook, 2ch, 3tr, 3tr in ring) 6 times, 5ch, dc in 3rd ch from hook, 2ch, ss in top st of 3-ch.

Round 2 Dc in next tr, (10ch, dc in centre tr of next group) 6 times, 10ch, ss in first dc. Fasten off.

Little wheel

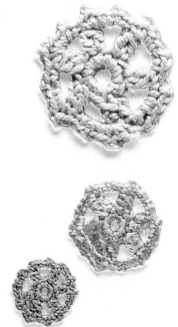

Size No. 1.25 crochet hook and very fine cotton produce a motif 2cm across.

Materials and uses Make tiny motifs from fine silky yarn or lurex to scatter around the neckline of an evening top, or use medium-weight cotton to decorate place mats and serviette holders.

Make 6ch and join into a ring with a ss into first ch.

Round 1 1ch, 12dc in ring, join with a ss to first dc.

Round 2 3ch, tr in same dc used for joining, *3ch, miss next dc, holding back on hook last loop of each tr make 2tr in next dc, yrh and draw through all 3 loops on hook – called cluster –; repeat from * 4 more times, 3ch, join with a ss to top of first tr.

Round 3 1ch, (dc, 2ch, dc) in each 3-ch space twice, join with a ss to first dc. Fasten off.

Crème de menthe

Size No. 2.50 crochet hook and fine cotton produce a motif 8.5cm across.

Materials and uses Use medium-weight yarn for random appliqué motifs on cushions, or use fine silky cotton to trim tablecloth or tray-cloth edges.

Make 10ch and join into a ring with a ss into first ch.

Round 1 4ch, 27dtr in ring, join with a ss to 4th st of 4-ch.

Round 2 Dc in same place as ss, *5ch, miss 1dtr, dc in next dtr; repeat from * around, ending with 1ch, dtr in first dc made.

Round 3 Ss in loop formed by 1-ch and dtr, 4ch, holding back on hook the last loop of each dtr make 3dtr in same loop, yarn over and draw through all loops on hook – a 3-dtr cluster made –, (7ch, 4-dtr cluster in next loop) 13 times, 7ch, ss into top of first cluster. Fasten off.

FRUIT & FLOWERS

Realistic three-dimensional designs can be achieved in crochet by using a bobble or embossed technique, or by working twice into the same round, or by joining two or more separate pieces. The fruit and flower patterns in this chapter range from tiny motifs like the Forget-me-not, p.90, *to larger designs such as the* Bunch of grapes, p.87. *These designs can be used to good effect singly, as brooches or to decorate haircombs, hatbands, lapels and pockets; they also look attractive when rows or clusters of them are used.*

Rose Red

Size No. 2.00 crochet hook and fine cotton produce a motif 5.5cm across.
Materials and uses Decorate a hatband with motifs made from fine cotton, or use silk thread for delicate flowers to trim a neck edge.

Make 8ch and join into a ring with a ss into first ch.
Round 1 6ch, *1tr in ring, 3ch; repeat from * 4 more times, 1ss into 3rd of 6ch.
Round 2 Into each space work 1dc, 1htr, 3tr, 1htr and 1dc (6 petals).
Round 3 *5ch, 1dc into next tr of round before last, inserting hook from back; repeat from * ending with 5ch.
Round 4 Into each space work 1dc, 1htr, 5tr, 1htr and 1dc.
Round 5 *7ch, 1dc into next dc of round before last, inserting hook from back; repeat from *ending with 7ch.
Round 6 Into each space work 1dc, 1htr, 7tr, 1htr and 1dc, 1ss into first dc. Fasten off.

Cherries

Size No. 2.00 crochet hook and fine cotton produce cherries 2.5cm across and leaves 2.5cm long.

Materials and uses Use medium-weight yarn for a pocket or lapel appliqué motif or decorate children's clothing with tiny cherries made from fine cotton.

This design uses 4 colours, A, B, C and D.

Background
Using A, make a round medallion as on p.63.

Berries
Using B, make 4ch.

Base row 8dtr into 4th ch from hook, turn.

Next row 3ch, *leaving last loop of each dtr on hook work 1dtr into each of next 5dtr − 5 loops on hook −, yrh, draw through all loops on hook; repeat from * once more. Fasten off. Make one more berry.

Leaves
Using C, make 8ch.

Next row 1dc into 2nd ch from hook, 1htr into next ch, 1tr into each of next 3ch, 1htr into next ch, 3dc into last ch, working down other side of ch, work 1htr into next ch, 1tr into each of next 3ch, 1htr into next ch, 1dc into last ch. Fasten off.

Make one more leaf in the same way. Sew leaves and berries on to background, padding berries with a small amount of spare yarn, and embroider stems with yarn D as illustrated.

Bunch of grapes

Size No. 4.00 crochet hook and double knitting wool produce a motif 15cm long, 8cm wide.

Materials and uses Use a single motif made from medium-weight yarn for a pocket appliqué, or use fine cotton to decorate place mats and serviette holders.

This design uses 2 colours, A and B.
Grapes
Using A, make 2ch.
Base row 3dc into 2nd ch from hook.
Next row 1ch, 1dc into first dc, leaving last loop of each st on hook work 5tr into next dc, yrh and draw through all loops on hook − called cluster −, 1dc into last dc, turn.
Next row 1ch, 2dc into first dc, 1dc into top of cl, 2dc into next dc, turn.
Next row 1ch, 1dc into first dc, (1 cluster into next dc, 1 dc into next dc) twice, turn (2 clusters).
Next row 1ch, 2dc into first dc, 1dc into each st to last dc, 2dc into last dc, turn (7dc).
Next row 1ch, 1 dc into first dc, *1 cluster into next dc, 1 dc into next dc; repeat from * to end, turn, (3 clusters). Repeat last 2 rows until there are 6 clusters.
Next row 1ch, miss first st, 1dc into

each of next 11sts, turn.
Next row 1ch, 1dc into first st, *1 cluster into next dc, 1 dc into next dc; repeat from * to end (5 clusters). Fasten off.
Leaf
Using B, make 7ch.
Base row 1dc into 2nd ch from hook, 1dc into each of next 5ch, turn.
Next row 1ch, 1dc into each of next 2dc, (1htr, 1tr) into next dc, (1tr, 1dtr, 3ch, 1dc) into next dc, (1htr, 1tr) into next dc, 3tr into dc at top of leaf, (1tr, 1htr) into next dc down second side of leaf, (1dc, 3ch, 1dtr, 1tr) into next dc, (1tr, 1htr) into next dc, 1dc into each of last 2dc. Fasten off. Make a second leaf in the same way, ending with 12ch for stalk, 1dc into 2nd ch from hook, 1dc into each ch to end. Fasten off.
Sew grapes to leaves and then use as an appliqué motif.

Poppy

Size No. 3.00 crochet hook and medium-weight yarn produce a flower 7cm across.

Materials and uses Embellish the edge of a pot plant holder with poppies made from fine cotton, or use several to decorate place mats and serviette holders.

This flower uses 2 colours, A and B. With A, make 6ch and join into a ring with a ss into first ch.

Round 1 1ch, 7dc into ring, 8dc, join with a ss to first ch.

Round 2 1ch, * 2dc into next dc; repeat from * to end, join with a ss to first ch (17dc).

Round 3 1ch, 16dc into ring, working into ring over first 2 rounds, join with a ss to first ch. Break off A.

Round 4 (petal) Join in B, 1ch, 1dc into each of next 4dc, turn, * 1ch, dc into st at base of ch, 1dc into each dc, 2dc into turning chain, *, turn; repeat from * to * once more, (9dc), work 2 rows straight on these dc, turn, 1 dc, work 2dc tog, 1dc into each of next 3dc, 2dc tog, 1dc into turning chain, turn, 1ch, 2dc tog, 1dc into next dc, 2dc tog, 1dc into turning chain, turn, omit 1ch and first dc, 1dc into each of next 2dc, 2dc tog. Fasten off.

Make 3 more petals in same way, beginning each petal in same place as last st of last petal and working last dc of last petal into same place as first on first petal.

Round 5 1ch, 1dc into each st round all petals. Break off B.

Round 6 (Stamens) Rejoin A round stem of any dc worked in last centre round, * 6ch, ss into 2nd ch and each ch to centre, dc round stem of next dc; repeat from * to end, join with a ss to first ch. Fasten off.

Daffodil

Size No. 3.00 crochet hook and medium-weight wool produce a flower 6.5cm across.

Materials and uses Decorate hair combs or hairslides with flowers made from fine cotton, or use wool or cotton crêpe for lapel or pocket motifs.

This flower uses 3 colours, A, B and C.

Using A, make 4ch and join into a ring with a ss into first ch.

Round 1 2ch to count as first htr, 5htr into ring, join with a ss to 2nd of first 2ch (6htr). Break off A.

Round 2 Join in B, ★ 7ch, 1dc into 3rd ch from hook, 1dc into each of next 4ch, 1ss into next dc, 1dc into next dc; repeat from ★ to end, join with a ss to first ch (3 petals), turn.

Round 3 1ch to count as first dc, 1dc into each of next 5dc working into back loop only of each st up side of petal, ★ (1dc, 1ch, 1dc) into top of petal, 6dc down side of petal, miss ss and next dc, 6dc up side of petal working into back loop only of each st; repeat from ★ once more, (1dc, 1ch, 1dc), 6dc down side of last petal, miss ss and last dc, join with a ss to first ch. Work into back loop only of each st from now on.

Round 4 1ch to count as first dc, ★ 1dc into each dc to top of petal, (1dc, 2ch, 1dc) into 1ch sp at top, 1dc into each dc to bottom of petal, miss 2 sts at base; repeat from ★ 3 more times, join with a ss to first ch.

Round 5 As round 4. Fasten off. This completes one petal section. Make another in the same way.

Round 6 With ridged side of flower facing and using C work under both loops of each st from now on in normal way, rejoin C to one half tr at centre of one petal section, 1ch to count as first dc, 1dc into st at base of ch, 2dc into each htr all round.

Round 7 ★ 1ch to count as first dc, 1dc into each dc to end, join with a ss to first ch.

Round 8 1ch to count as first dc, 1dc into st at base of ch, ★ 1dc into each of next 2dc, 2dc into next dc; repeat from ★ to last 2 sts, 1dc into each of next 2sts, join with a ss to first ch.

Round 9 As round 7.

Round 10 2ch to count as first dc and picot point, 1ss into 2nd ch from hook, ★ 1dc into next dc, 1ch, 1ss into top of st just worked; repeat from ★ to end, join with a ss to first ch. Fasten off.

To finish Sew second petal section to first so that petals lie between petals of first section.

Forget-me-not

Size No. 3.00 crochet hook and medium-weight wool produce a flower 3.5cm across.

Materials and uses Use glitter yarn for random appliqué motifs scattered over an evening shawl, or use fine cotton for a pretty border around a tray cloth.

This flower uses 2 colours, A and B. Using A, make 6ch and join into a ring with a ss into first ch.

Round 1 1ch, 8dc in ring, join with a ss to back loop of first dc. Break off A.

Round 2 Join in B, *3ch, holding back on hook the last loop of each tr make 3tr in same back loop where last ss was made, yarn over and draw through all 4 loops on hook − called cluster −, 3ch, ss in same back loop, ss in back loop of next dc; repeat from * around, ending with ss in same back loop where last cluster was made (8 petals made).

Round 3 Working in front loops of dcs on round 1, ss in front loop of first dc, 5ch, ss in 3rd ch from hook − called picot −, * htr in front loop of next dc, 3ch, complete a picot; repeat from * around (8 picots), join with a ss to 2nd ch of 5-ch at beginning of round. Fasten off.

ANIMALS & OBJECTS

*Most of the patterns in this section are given in chart form,
read the chart upwards from the bottom right hand corner.
These designs are particularly suitable for children's
articles, but using squared paper and a little imagination it
is easy to design your own patterns. Remember to keep the
design simple, without too many colour changes.*

Gingerbread man

Size No. 2.50 crochet hook and double knitting yarn produce a motif
10cm wide and 12cm high.
Materials and uses Decorate a child's pinafore or dungarees with a
motif made from machine-washable yarn, or use fine or very fine
cotton and sew a string of tiny gingerbread men around the hem or
neck of a sweater.

Make 20 ch.
Base row 1tr into 4th ch from hook,
1tr into each ch to end, turn (18tr).
Next row Ss over 6tr, 3ch, miss next
tr, 1tr into each of next 5tr, turn.
Next row 3ch, miss first tr, 1tr into
each of next 5tr, turn.
Next row (legs) 3ch, miss first tr, 1tr
into each of next 2tr, turn, 3ch.
Work 3 rows in tr on these 3tr.
Fasten off. Rejoin yarn at beginning
of legs and work another leg to match
first.
Head With right side facing, rejoin
yarn to 8th tr along 'arms', 3ch, miss

first tr, 1tr into each of next 3tr, turn.
Next row 3ch, 1tr into first tr, 2tr
into each tr to end, turn.
Next row 3ch, miss first tr, 1tr into
each tr to end, turn.
Next row 2ch, 1tr in next tr, *(yrh,
insert hook into next tr, yrh, draw
lp through, yrh, draw through 2 lps)
twice, yrh, draw through all lps on
hook; rep from * to end, turn.
Work 1 row of dc all around gingerbread man. Fasten off.
To finish Using an oddment of black
yarn, embroider eyes, mouth and
buttons as illustrated.

Duck

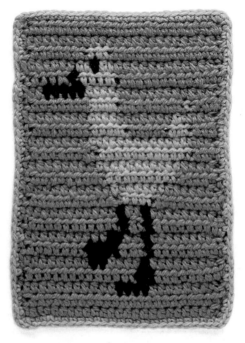

Size No. 3.00 crochet hook and double knitting yarn produce a rectangle 14cm by 19cm.

Materials and uses Use chunky or double knitting yarn for a blanket, or make dungaree pockets from machine-washable yarn.

This design uses 3 colours, A, B and C.

Note *To change colour, before drawing through last 2 loops of last tr of one colour group, drop this colour, pick up the other colour, yarn over and draw through the 2 loops on hook. Continue with other colour, carrying the dropped colour along top of previous row and working over it to conceal it.*

Using A, make 27ch.

Row 1 Tr in 4th ch from hook and in each ch across (25tr, counting turning ch as 1tr), 3ch, turn.

Row 2 Tr in each tr, tr in top st of turning ch.

Row 3 Holding yarn B along top of previous row, with A tr in 9tr (thus concealing B), changing yarn in last tr. With yarn B tr in 4tr, carrying yarn A concealed in trs and changing yarn at last tr. With yarn A tr in 12tr,

3ch, turn.

Rows 4–25 Continue following chart, carrying unused yarn and changing yarn as in row 3.

To finish Using C, work one row of double crochet all around the edge.

Each square represents 1tr

Row 1

Teddy bear

Size No. 3.00 crochet hook and medium-weight yarn produce a square 16cm across.

Materials and uses Make a pram cover using wool crêpe or medium-weight yarn, or sew four or more squares together for cushions for a child's room.

This design uses 3 colours, A, B and C.

Note *To change colour, before drawing through last 2 loops of last tr of one colour group, drop this colour, pick up the other colour, yarn over and draw through the 2 loops on hook. Continue with other colour, carrying the dropped colour along top of previous row and working over it to conceal it.*

Using A, make 42ch.

Row 1 Tr in 4ch from hook and in each ch across (40tr, counting turning chain as 1tr), 3ch, turn.

Rows 2 and 3 Tr in each tr, tr in top st of turning chain, 3ch, turn.

Row 4 Holding yarn B along top of previous row, with yarn A tr in 3tr (thus concealing yarn B), changing colour in the last tr. With yarn B tr in 6tr, carrying yarn A concealed in trs and changing colour in the last tr. With yarn A tr in 20tr, carrying yarn B concealed in trs and changing colour in last tr. With yarn B tr in 6tr, carrying yarn A concealed in trs

and changing colours in last tr. With yarn A tr in 4tr, 3ch, turn.

Rows 5–20 Continue following chart, introducing yarn C and carrying unused yarn and changing yarn as in row 4.

To finish Work a row of double crochet edging all around, and embroider eyes, nose and mouth as illustrated.

Each square represents 2tr

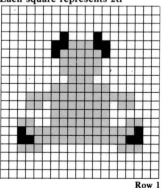

Row 1

Butterfly

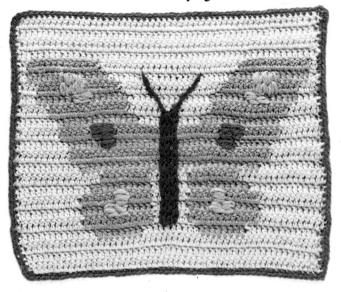

Size No. 3.00 crochet hook and medium-weight yarn produce a rectangle 20cm by 16cm.

Materials and uses Make a rug from chunky yarn, alternating butterfly squares with plain squares, or use thick cotton yarn for place mats, working each mat in different shades.

This design uses 4 colours, A, B, C and D.

Note *To change colour, before drawing through last 2 loops of last tr of one colour group, drop this colour, pick up the other colour, yarn over and draw through the 2 loops on hook. Continue with other colour, carrying the dropped colour along top of previous row and working over it to conceal it.*

Using A, make 56ch.

Row 1 Tr in 4th ch from hook and in each ch across (54tr, counting turning ch as 1tr), 3ch, turn.

Row 2 Tr in each tr, tr in top st of turning ch.

Row 3 As row 2.

Row 4 Holding yarn B along top of previous row, with A tr in 14tr (thus concealing B), changing yarn in last tr. With yarn B tr in 8tr, carrying yarn A concealed in trs and changing yarn in last tr. With yarn A tr in 10tr, carrying yarn B concealed in trs and changing colour in the last tr. With

yarn B tr in 8tr, carrying yarn A concealed in trs and changing colours in last tr. With A tr in 14tr, 3ch, turn.

Rows 5–23 Continue following chart, carrying unused yarn and changing yarn as in row 4.

To finish Using C and D embroider body, antennae, and pattern on wings. Work one row of double crochet all around the edge.

Each square represents 2tr

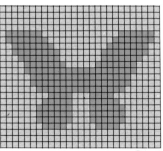

Row 1

Index

A

Abbreviations   20
Animals and objects   91–94
  Butterfly   94
  Duck   92
  Gingerbread man   91
  Teddy bear   93

B

Bar and lattice   11
Basic stitch variations   12
Basic stitches   10
Basic techniques   7
Beginning a round   13
Blocking   15
Bobble stitch   12
Borders   16
Bullion stitch   12

C

Cabling around stitch   12
Calculating number of medallions   17
Chain stitch   9
Circles, layout of   18
Circles and octagons   63–78
  Butterfly wings   68
  Catherine wheel   65
  English rose   73
  Filet octagon   67
  Floral ring   75
  Golden wheel   74
  Lemon and lime   64
  Peach sorbet   64
  Plain circle   63
  Prairie rose   72
  Ridged octagon   78
  Ruby wine   71
  Satellite   74
  Scallops and circles   70
  Spinning wheel   69
  Striped octagon   66
  Sunburst   76
  Wheel lace   77
Colourwork   14
Counting   9
Crossed double crochet   12

D

Double chain stitch   9
Double crochet   10
Double crochet border   16
Double crochet ring   13
Double treble   11

E

Ending a round   14

F

Fillers   16
Fillers and motifs   79–84
  Big wheel   82
  Cactus flower   81
  Crème de menthe   84
  Daisy chain   80
  Green florette   82
  Little wheel   83
  Powder blue   83
  Starfish   79
  Tumbleweed   81
Finishing off   9
Foundation chain   9
Fringed border   16
Fruit and flowers   85–90
  Bunch of grapes   87
  Cherries   86
  Daffodil   89
  Forget-me-not   90
  Poppy   88
  Rose red   85

H

Half treble   10
Hexagons   45–58
  Afghan Hexagon   57
  Anemone   48
  Blue belle   46
  Cobweb   58
  Flower hexagon   56
  Hidden petals   55
  Little spindles   52
  Ornate hexagon   50
  Pinwheel   49
  Ribbed hexagon   45
  Rosette   54
  Snowflake   53
  Spoked hexagon   51
  Tinkerbell   47
Hexagons, layout of   18
Holding the hook and yarn   8
Hook and yarn guide   20
Hooks   7

J

Joining   15, 16
Joining in new colours   14, 15

O

Octagons, layout of   19
Openwork stitches   11

S

Seams   15, 16
Securing loose ends   14
Single chain ring   13
Single crochet   10
Size guide   17, 20
Slip stitch   10
Squares 21–44
  Afghan square   44
  Arched square   27
  Bermuda triangle   24
  Bull's eye   28
  Cartwheel   29
  Crossed square   26
  Daisy square   23
  Diamond lattice   38
  Flower square   41
  Irish lace square   34
  Lacy daisy   39
  Lacy shells   42
  Lattice square   43
  Lattice star   36
  Lazy daisy   26
  Petal square   40
  Plain square   30
  Powder puff   31
  Rainbow   22
  Sea green square   33
  Sparkle star   37
  Square in a square   35
  Squares and triangles   32
  Star bright   25
  Tudor rose   21
  Wagon wheel   30
Squares, layout of   19

T

Textured stitches   12
Threading yarn   8
Treble   10
Triangles 59–62
  Crossed triangle   61
  Eternal triangle   60
  Lace triangle   59
  Shell triangle   60
  Tricorn   62
Triple treble   11
Turning chains   9

W

Working in the round   13

Y

Yarn   7

Acknowledgements

Samples
June Briggs

Artist
John Hutchinson

Photographer
Ian O'Leary

Typesetting
Cambrian Typesetters

Reproduction
· Newsele SRL